Praise for *Fourteen Hills*

"Beautifully designed, impeccably edited, *Fourteen Hills* is one of those handful of literary journals doing the important work of keeping American writing alive and new."
George Saunders, author of *In Persuasion Nation*

"The journal is something of a collage itself, boasting a variety of talented writers from San Francisco and around the world."
Jennifer Gomoll, *NewPages.com*

"[*Fourteen Hills*] blends the traditional litmag with experimental writing in a slick, well-produced journal."
Todd Dayton, *MetroACTIVE*

"Smart, quirky, literate—every piece in this journal gives the reader a juicy nugget to sink their teeth into, and something meaty that sticks to the mind's ribs."
David Henry Sterry, author of *Chicken*

Vol. 18 No. 2

2012

Acknowledgements.

Fourteen Hills would like to thank the following for help and support in putting this issue together:

Maxine Chernoff
Barbara Eaton
Wix Lounge
SB Stokes
Jennifer Daly
Karl Frauhammer
Chet Wiener

Fourteen Hills would like to thank the following businesses and individuals for their generous donations to our fundraising events:
222 Hyde Street, Almanac Beer Company, Amazon, Ayuna Collins, Borderland Books, Cafe Metropol, Francoise Lajoie Brunette, Funky Door Yoga, Park Chow, Philz Coffee, Rock Canyon Leather, Safeway, Sam Schwartz, Tartine Bakery, Whole Foods, Zunki.

Credits.

Book Layout and Design: Kelly McNerney and Miah Jeffra
Cover and Art Design: Miah Jeffra, Kelly McNerney, Jason R. Schenheit
Copy Editors: Keely Hyslop, Kelly McNerney, LeAnne Milway Chabalko, Diana Rosinus, Sandra Wassilie,
Cover Artwork: Gilda Davidian, "You and I," digital print.

Distribution.

Small Press Distribution, Berkeley, California / www.spdbooks.org
Ubiquity Distributors, Inc., Brooklyn, New York / www.ubiquitymags.com

ISSN: 1085-4576
ISBN: 978-1-889292-54-0

Fourteen Hills is published by the Creative Writing Department at San Francisco State University, with the support of the Instructionally Related Activities Fund.

Vol.18 No.2
2012

Fourteen Hills is published twice yearly in San Francisco, California

Subscriptions:
Individual – One year for $15. Two years for $28.
Institutional – One year for $17. Two years for $32.
Single issues $9.

Submissions should be accompanied by a self-addressed, stamped envelope. Writers may submit once per submission period. Submission periods are: September 1 to January 1 for inclusion in the spring issue (released in May) and March 1 to July 1 for inclusion in the winter issue (released in December). All correspondence should be addressed to the appropriate editor at *Fourteen Hills*, c/o the Creative Writing Department, San Francisco State University, 1600 Holloway Ave., San Francisco, CA 94132. Details at 14hills.net.

Contents.

Fourteen Hills

THE SAN FRANCISCO STATE UNIVERSITY REVIEW

When the Ship Disappeared from View

Eliza Rotterman

It fell from the edge of the world and on fishless shores of distant stars angels wept: what had been contained was now endless. Belief sailed through the body to an eternity of waiting, of circling, became a theory about ending where one began, a story in which you traveled west, your heart a slender memory of all the rooms in which it sang. And in singing, it woke you to the mystery of *nothing comes from nothing*, to the distance between what happened and how it would be remembered. What happened is the ratio of heat to skin to clouds tamping out the stars, a map cracking into a thousand autumn pieces, roads pouring forth the liquid slide of destiny. But you remember looking into the southern stretch of the Milky Way, glimpsing beyond the pinwheeling arm into a room gone dark. A room in which the story has just been read and drifting among the remnants of stars and ships you find yourself at the edge of the world surprised by how little holds you back. The soul like the moon passes in and out of form, of light. Or not at all. You read, *the future stands fixed but we move in infinite space* and the arrow arcs towards the sun. When the story in which one returns became a story in which one doesn't, you went further, seeking the stormy tip of the jetty, for you were the palm of the collective, its will outstretching your fingers. Belief is the arc an object makes when force defies gravity. It is the reason you left. And keep leaving. It is an equation expressed by division and progressively shorter distances. This morning a ship nearing shore returned you to you, but only for a moment before passing through to the other side.

In a Word

Rick Crabtree

He tells me it's not anchored in a story,
that it lacks the initiative a verb might give it,
that without a tree or a purple old lady
   the words just hang there waiting.
For what he doesn't know, so he wants
   to turn the page,
wants to tell me to find a home for it
   in this world,
as if the words we have are the product
   of something else,
like those words, without
   a train conductor or the smell of burning
   and the whine of hogs cooking inside
   are things from unreality.
Like a rain drop could fall from a tree and not
   shake a leaf.
That fish out of water has a story,
   even if it's only bones when we find it.

Song of the Cosmogonist

Matthew Gagnon

It's not the proof
but the passage
holding you skyward

when all the underwood
is beginning to rot.

Looking glass blue,
every captive bray
is translated from you.

The booming intonation
of hymn, hallo, hello

throbs in its panic
with all the leaf stammer
and fathered trefoil.

When the dilating globe
is an anthem of you

it fetches the heady
boom of liberty
like a final discourse.

Distant Planets

Suzanne Barnecut

My husband is tired of hearing about my teeth. "I'm going to leave," he says while putting his laundry away. I've folded his shirts into piles, arranged by color, light to dark, and paired his socks into neat couplets. This is how easy I've made it for him, but I make a mental note to take him seriously, because it is serious—my teeth are vital, and so is my marriage. Even as he talks of leaving, what he's doing is the opposite.

I stand there with my arms crossed. I don't mean to be so closed off, so I untangle myself and feel apelike, arms idle and heavy at my sides. I feel the weight of them tugging against my shoulder, feel how tight the muscles are, pulling my neck and jawline, and I bring a hand to my mandible and wonder about the strain on my roots. He's saying, "You have to love me more than you love your teeth. You know that, right? It's a reasonable question. It's more than reasonable."

I nod. The question is logical. I know this.

"So do you?"

"Of course I love you." This is where I should stop, but I can't help myself. I feel the need to explain that it's not a competition, or it doesn't have to be. I want him to see that we're talking about two different things. "I fear for my teeth. I love you. Get it?"

We're facing each other but the bed is between us, a demilitarized zone that neither of us will cross. He's looking for me to meet his gaze, but looking at him makes it hard to think so I look elsewhere, behind him. On the top of the armoire is a charcoal sketch of a ballerina that we bought at an estate sale, her diaphanous tulle skirt spread wide. It once hung over an old woman's bed. We thought it was sad, probably her favorite picture, left behind. In a way, we imagined it as her companion, and now we thought of it as ours.

"Will you look at me?" I hear the frustration in his voice, but I can't. I'm at the dresser, removing my earrings, the ones he hates because the backs are sharp and they poke at him when we lie close. He sighs, a long breath leaving him. "You obsess," he says, "and you need help."

"No, what I need is a new dentist. That will fix everything. I need someone who will support me."

My husband takes his pillow and heads for the living room. There's no use going after him. I begin my nightly routine: first a thorough flossing and tooth count, then the water pick. I brush every tooth three times with the electric toothbrush in a circular motion, almost like I'm polishing them, always left to right, top to bottom, front to back. I check my gums for recession. Then I floss again, water pick one last time for good measure, and rinse with prescription mouthwash. It takes a half hour, not too bad.

When I'm alone in bed, I run my fingers over the enamel surface of my teeth and feel how clean and slick they are. I feel confident that nothing is lodged between them, breeding rot, causing a stress fracture. I can sleep peacefully knowing they are safe.

◊

He leaves twelve days later, waits until after I get home from the grocery store. He waits so that I will see him standing in the hallway in his long coat with three suitcases, a backpack, and his computer bag—a picture of a man who has reached his limit, except that he is too young and should still have some fight.

I put the grocery bags on the floor. "Where are you going?"

"A hotel," he says. "Rachael, I can't do this anymore." I want to know what *this* means exactly. That he's really serious I'm starting to understand.

"What is this? A break? A separation? What are you asking me to do in order for you to stay?"

"I'm not asking for anything." He's standing so close that I can see his slate blue eyes go glassy, spill over. I feel like I might cry too. It's hard to breathe. I put my palm on his chest to lean in for support, but he takes a step backward. "No," he says. "That's not true. I'm asking you for a divorce."

I know this is the wrong response, not at all what I mean to do, but my stubbornness, like my compulsions, is hard to overcome. I open the front door and gesture as though to say: please, after you. Have a nice life.

Once he's left, once his bags have all been moved to the courtyard and then into a waiting taxi, once the door is locked behind him, I feel as though I will be crushed by the emptiness, as though all the air molecules, so many, uninterrupted now and free to rush down the hallway and through empty rooms, will push against my hollows and flatten me into nothing. I imagine all that will be left of me when he returns are my teeth, a gleaming pile on the wooden floor.

Days later, evidence of him is everywhere: the fridge, the fruit bowl. I don't know what to do with his food. It is almost like he's died. It's like I'm grieving, and yet somehow there is also a freedom, a lifting. There's no more yelling over my dental work, over the bills and insurance. I panic for a moment about the insurance. He has very good insurance. Will he take that from me?

I eat only soft things, cereal bars and protein shakes, bananas and yogurt—but only after the yogurt has set out so that it's not too cold. I love string cheese and will never eat caramel or salt water taffy. Corn cobs give me nightmares, and things with sharp bones, whole skeletons still inside. I don't drink coffee. But my husband does. I am at a loss when I see all the things I bought for him: the tortilla chips and carrots and the Gala apples, the ones he likes best, with their beautiful skin, constellations of golden stars in red galaxies.

We are too young to get divorced. This feels like a fact. We are each twenty-seven and we've been married just over three years. We celebrated our last anniversary at an Italian restaurant where I ordered spaghetti without garlic, tossed in olive oil and finely shaved parmesan, no pepper. I celebrated with a glass of white wine. My husband had the chicken piccata and toasted garlic bread. "To us," we said, raising our glasses. We looked each other in the eye, like you're supposed to, like you mean it. I expect that our friends will push us towards marriage counseling. Surely someone will convince him that this is necessary. Our friends don't know about my teeth, and now he will tell them. He will air our secrets because he is no longer their protector. Suddenly it will all make sense, that I do not have an eating disorder or even a very picky palate. I decide I won't tell anyone about the separation, that there is no need for anyone to know. Instead I play at widow, unsure and oddly curious about how it feels to be left with myself.

◊

My lawyer is a beautiful woman named LaGretta. She wears tailored suits, always with skirts and tall heels. Her name reminds me of the word regret, and she is all business but not unkind. She has an air of authority. "I'll take care of you," she said during our first meeting, and what she meant was that I'll have what I need when all of this is done. It is almost a lie because, of course, I will need my husband.

"As you can see," he says, "she has beautiful teeth."

It's explained to the lawyers that I've had six root canals, seven fillings, and three bridges. I get regular deep cleanings beneath my gums. I had one tooth forcibly removed. I get x-rays twice as often as required because a year is really too long to wait and see if cavities or hairline fractures have manifested. I've seen the dentist—or rather, three different dentists—a total of seventy-five times in fifteen months. I spent ten thousand dollars on dental work. Put that way, it does sound like a lot.

The office belongs to my husband's lawyer. There's a long conference table, everything a dark redwood, reminding me of blood, which reminds me of the dream I had the night before. In the dream I'd wandered into a large public restroom, through a maze of stalls, each with a door that didn't lock or a toilet that had not been flushed. Every toilet bowl was filled with blood.

"You do realize," LaGretta says to me, gently, "that ten thousand dollars is a lot of money for non-emergency dental work."

I nod peaceably, feeling my husband's eyes on me, though I don't appreciate her taking his side. I wonder how this contributes to her taking care of me unless it is in a more elemental way, motherly.

"In just one year," my husband adds for good measure. His lawyer, a very thin man, puts his hand on my husband's forearm. He means for my husband to shut up, but it looks like he's hanging on for dear life.

When I try to make eye contact with my husband, I can see that he's not open for business. He's decided that this is what he wants, that he is safer this way. He will be loved better by someone else, he's thinking, and this makes me angry. It seems very selfish.

"I might be pregnant," I say. The room goes silent, and everyone, even LaGretta, stares.

The thin lawyer clears his throat. "How do you know? Have you taken a test?" I can see that he is a man predisposed not to like me. I can see that he finds me absurd.

"No." I match his tone, even and cool. "I dreamt about blood. It's very common for pregnant women to dream of blood."

"Okay," LaGretta says, putting papers into her monogrammed briefcase, snapping it shut. "Why don't we take a break? Let's set up another meeting. We'll have this all resolved by then."

My husband says nothing. Not a thing, but he stares after me, mouth agape. It *is* possible I could be pregnant. It's not like my teeth kept me from making love.

Later he calls to ask, "What was that?" I am painting my nails, so I lay the phone on the bathroom tile. I have a red color called "Wife Goes On" that I considered, given the circumstances, but instead went with a cool gray-lavender called "St. Lucia Lilac." I put him on speaker so that his voice echoes around me and fills the room in a nice way. A candle on the windowsill casts warm light against the walls and where the mirror is splintered, the reflection multiplies into a chorus of quivering flame.

"I don't know if it's a good idea for us to be talking." I say this even though I want desperately to talk to him. I'd like to say normal things, about how I was passed over for promotion to floor manager. I work in a bookstore, one of the big ones where you can drink coffee and sit in armchairs. "You're so exacting," my boss said to counter my disappointment, meaning, I know, that she'd prefer me to continue shelving the go-backs, keeping the store in perfect order. She doesn't want me handling unhappy customers, deciding when to give discounts, or counting all the cash in the tills. I wanted to say, "I need this. I'm getting divorced," but that would be a cheap trick, and would also make the divorce a thing that might really happen. I want to tell him that I'd like him to come home, but I know I can't give him what he wants, at least not right away.

"Really," he says. "Why would you say such a thing?" There is a pleading sound in his voice, and I imagine his vocal chords as long ribbons, stretched out. His teeth have never bothered me. A relief, he used to say. He didn't need to brush them before we kissed. If there was food stuck there, if he forgot to floss at night, it wasn't my concern. His teeth were his business. Mine were mine.

"Because it might be true."

"Based on a dream?"

"Yes."

"You're crazy," he says. I hear him open and close a door. I start at this.

"I'm not. You know I'm not. Don't say that." I've had premonitions that have come true. He knows this. I have predicted earthquakes. I'm good with horse races, lucky. "It's my body," I say. "I think I know it."

"You need to take a test. I don't want our child to watch you obsess. It isn't normal. It isn't healthy."

"You can't take away things that I don't even have yet," I yell before pushing the end button carefully with my wet fingernail. But I wonder whether he can.

There is still a lot in the house that belongs to him, not just food, slowly spoiling. He left his toothbrush, for one thing. His treadmill and hand weights, his books and CDs. Clothes he doesn't want are still in the closet, like they're my problem now. Camping gear and tools are still in our garage. I don't think he cares about wedding gifts, silver-edged plates. There are also all his rocks. He's a geologist, with some background in paleogeology, meaning very old rocks, though he's early in his career and mostly helps others with their research. His passion for rocks is why we had to live in this particular neighborhood, because it was on firm bedrock. Outside we have a rock garden, and some of these rocks have made it into the house as paper weights, or as marvels on bookshelves or windowsills. There is a beautiful gray granite stone next to the kitchen sink. He can point at any rock and say with impressive immediacy whether it's basalt or quartz, claystone or oil shale. He knows every type of rock, and I think we must own a sample of each. Like him, I know every tooth, what number it is, its scientific name, but teeth don't bring me pleasure in the way that my husband's rocks do. Teeth cause me pain and then bring me solace. The rocks, they fascinate my husband and incite wonder. It's something different. I consider putting them all into a large trash bag and letting them sink into the river, to eventually wear down into sand. Or else gluing them together into a big rock wall so that I can continue to enjoy them and he will have to leave them behind. But either way it's too much work, so I do nothing.

When he first proposed, he said, "I have a rock for you," and held out a diamond. It was exactly the kind of thing I'd expect him to say, and I waited to hear about how it had once been made of coal, but instead he said that it wasn't just a rock he was giving me. It was an entire planet.

"It's true," he went on. "There is a diamond planet 4,000 light years away, and it's yours. I'm claiming it, if you'll marry me." This was all adorable and rehearsed, and of course the planet was too far away, and so all he had to offer was this small replica, this semblance of a planet.

He had not made this story up. A smaller diamond was inlaid into the platinum band, representing the neutron star around which the real diamond planet orbited. The diamond planet almost had what it needed to foster life. There was oxygen, maybe even hydrogen and helium. It wasn't that my husband was trying to give me the world. That wasn't what he was trying to say. He meant that there was potential in this place he'd discovered, room for possibility and growth.

I imagined my planet sparkling out there, a bright spot so far into the darkness that no one would ever be able to see it. I liked how it would remain mine that way. But this was when my husband thought my teeth were cute and that my nighttime routine was just a funny little quirk, maybe even healthy. So you like to keep your teeth clean, he'd say. There are worse problems.

He'd urge me to tell him the most awful thing that could happen.

It was a game, a kind of flirting, because he thought my answers were funny, or because like all men, instead of listening, he paused while I spoke and then offered a solution. He made things sound simple and uncomplicated, like my own mind had taken a vacation. He once shoved a poppyseed muffin under my nose and said, "I'm trying to understand. What would happen if you ate this?"

"The seeds," I answered, pointing at the spaces between my teeth, those vortexes for small particles of food. "They'll wedge there."

"So? What then?"

"I might break a filling."

"You can get fillings fixed. That's the beauty of dentists." It always ended this way, with him triumphant. Like, *voila*, done!

But it wasn't that easy. Life never was so easy, was it? Maybe that's what he didn't understand. I feared losing my teeth. I feared decay, that their foothold would loosen and they would all fall out. I feared dentures, clamming around with a toothless, gummy mouth. I feared how ugly I would be then and how no one would love me.

◊

It's true that when I was eleven, my brother knocked out my front tooth. I was hugging my mother and he came running down the hall too fast, his body trailing his open arms. His fist connected with my mouth, my tooth hurtled down my throat, and I swallowed it. Later, after I was cleaned up and drinking milk through a straw, my brother laughed and said, "You look funny." Then my father laughed, and next my mother, and they all thought it was apparently the funniest thing in the world that I had a lateral incisor knocking around my stomach and a gaping, dark wound in plain sight.

Still, I know it was a minor incident of my childhood and should not have made me so conscious of my mouth, thinking all the time of my teeth and how to protect them. It makes me worry now about the small thing that might be growing in my womb, all the missteps and accidents in life that can forever shape a person.

Three days before he left, my husband threw my toothbrush and water pick into the garbage where they would obviously be ruined. On the bathroom counter was a single new toothbrush, soft bristled, a tube of basic cavity-protection Colgate, and some floss—Walgreens brand, nothing special, not even mint-flavored. When I saw this, I threw his razor against the mirror, cracking the glass down the center in a jagged, lightning-like line. "What are you trying to do to me?" I yelled, feeling very much like a child, ashamed, but also like an animal directly threatened.

He took a hard stance. "You can do this. Brush like I would. You have five minutes." He removed his watch and held it out in front of him. "Get going," he said, "you're wasting time."

It was nothing short of an act of courage to hold the regular toothbrush, feeling the lack of power behind it, just my arm. There was only enough time for one pass over my teeth, a record-breaking flossing, and a quick rinse. Then he took it all away. "See," he said, grinning. "You did it."

I'd made him proud, but I felt awful. I burst into deep, shuddering sobs and woke that night from a dream in which my gums were festering and swollen.

In the evenings I take walks. I'm left at odds without my husband so I try to notice things, to get outside myself. I can do that. I focus on the details, as though someone will quiz me later about what I saw while out: a house sheathed entirely in bougainvillea vines, those ruby-colored, paper-thin flowers; a golden Buddha in a dark window, flanked by two burnished brass owls, lotus flowers at their feet made of wax and glass. At the preschool I put my eye to the window and see children's dioramas lined against a wall. The nearest one makes no sense. It contains a scene from the ocean with blue water and fish, and also an oversized gorilla made of plastic, its arms raised in strength or victory. It probably means something, and makes me think that I know this child. I know about disproportion.

It's not like I can't see the soft edges. It's not like my compulsions structure my whole world in black and white. I wasn't the only one to bring rigidity to the marriage. Really, I don't live by many rules, only a few. My husband is the one who takes measurements, who is exacting in his own ways. He too has daily routines, a rhythm.

My compulsions are more like the deep blue-gray of a distant shore, a place never traveled to but that seems familiar. They are siren songs. They are neither a coming or going but sometimes a barreling down, like a runaway bicycle on a steep incline, and at other times like the moment of crescendo in a song, a building anxiety that reaches a climax and then fades away, deeply satisfying. It's a dark forest that I live in, as though I'm always lost at night desperately seeking the moon. Everyone's world is like this: specific. My husband inhabits a space like the Southwest, with red mesas and plateaus, and the dark and rising shapes of pinnacle rocks against the open sky. There are agave flowers there. His is a beautiful space, all earth and air and light.

When the fog is too thick or wet, I give up and walk home. The fog itself is a marvel, but not in some metaphoric way. We live on a peninsula, and so the water can't help but thicken, rise, and move east. Still it is striking, even after seeing it every day. I suppose it is like this with any darkness. The fog creeps over edges of buildings, occluding their sharp corners, and makes parts of the city disappear entirely. It makes my own house seem inviting and warm; a window lit from within appears against the oncoming night as a square of honeyed light.

Post-marriage, my first dentist was a woman. Dr. Rivers was a keen business woman. It was what I liked about her. She would have made a good plastic surgeon. She was the kind of woman who understood that we all make choices, and were free to sink our own boats. When my husband realized I was undergoing enamel restoration ("For cariogenicity," I told him, meaning tooth decay), he gave me a strange look. "I don't understand," he said. "You take such good care."

He wanted to come with me and speak with Dr. Rivers directly. They moved into the next exam room but I could still hear. "I've only done what your wife asked," she said.

"You're telling me you're *removing* the enamel?" he said. "It can't be necessary. I've read up on this. Consider who I married. Her teeth are fine."

"Yes," she said. "It's a preventative restoration to protect your wife against future decay." She very calmly explained what I already knew. Enamel can be removed before decay is present. Dr. Rivers was placing dental sealants in the deepest fissures and grooves of my teeth, which we'd spent several visits carefully identifying.

"I'm suing for malpractice," he said before pulling me up from the chair by my elbow and out the door with my dental bib still on.

"What is wrong with you?" I said, trying to shake free.

"We're not paying for this visit," he yelled loud enough that Dr. Rivers would hear.

It was the first major fight of our marriage—of our whole relationship, really, which had, end to end, been short. "You've ruined it," I said. "Now I won't be able to go back."

"We'll find you someone who will only do the work you really need," he said once we had calmed, trying to be sympathetic. He thought I'd been victimized.

The dentist he found for me was prudent, an older gentleman near the end of his practice with a long alcohol-veined nose and ears whose length betrayed him as elderly. He liked to treat children, kept a large aquarium in the exam room and beneath it a cardboard treasure chest filled with plastic toys. "Is that sanitary?" I asked about the fish tank.

"Quite," he said. He did not need my money or my over-wrought worry. When I asked for him to remove my second premolar, he said, "Now why would I do that?"

I watched little angel fish swim around between underwater ferns past a sunken pirate ship. "It's crowding the others, putting pressure on them. It's making my whole mouth hurt." It wasn't true exactly. Premolars are bicuspids, and this means that they have two points, like a moon in its crescent stage. The space between each cusp was a ripe home for food to settle into, a particularly deep valley and thus, a risk. I also wanted the tip of my #26 lateral incisor shaved down. It came to a sharper V than the others and if I bit my lip it sometimes broke the skin. He said no to this as well. I can still remember his face as he shook it, the look of sadness there. It was the face of a captain who has realized he's going down with his ship, the inevitability of it. "I'm afraid I can't help you," he said.

The third dentist, a Dr. Wally—Wally being his first name, short for Wallace—removed the tooth because he knew, as I did, it wouldn't hurt anything to take it out. "It won't do any good either," he said, to be clear. I came home with a gauze-filled mouth, unable to eat, feeling wonderful. My husband assumed the tooth had been bad, that there had been some validity to my fears. I told him a story I'd recently read in *People* magazine, pretending it was my own: that I was very ill as an infant and had a fever of 105. As a result, my teeth grew in without enamel. They were all removed and replaced with a row of miniature silver teeth until my adult teeth grew in. I conjured the shame I imagined a child of five would feel, taunted by other children. It was the story my husband had been waiting for. I was finally letting him in to the inner recesses of my heart. "You poor thing," he said, taking me into his arms. "I couldn't have endured so much pain." We did very well for a while after that, and my follow-up dental visits were never questioned.

◊

One night the following week, my husband lets himself in with his house key, carrying a small brown paper bag. I'm watching *Castle* on TV, the crime-solving show where the handsome mystery novelist trails the attractive investigator, tormenting her and solving all her cases, usually by accident, because he's done something inappropriate and hapless. I like these shows, how the end is never what you expect, seeing how the forensic scientists work. They use teeth when they can for DNA, to identify a body. In the same way, the rocks my husband studies also reveal more than you might imagine. He can look closely and see a stone's composition, its age, and what part of the world it came from, what the conditions were like then. At times we'd joked that our fascinations were parallel—or rather, not the fascinations but the subjects. Rocks and teeth were both specimens containing valuable information that might be useful years later.

"You're back," I say. I am surprised at the sound of my voice, the rush of warmth there, the relief I feel. He stands in front of the television, looking well. He is not gaunt or drawn.

"I need to know if I'm going to be a father," he says, unearthing one of those e.p.t. boxes with more than one test inside. The truth is that we'd wanted children—both of us—but the more we argued, the more our ideas about the future began to fade. I feel a rising hope at the sight of him, at the thought of coming together and refocusing, but also an ache that is a lot like premenstrual cramping. "I'll have no chance at custody if I file for divorce knowing there's a baby."

My anger flares, and the happy image of our rekindling dissipates. "I'm not taking a test. You can't make me."

I know what he's thinking when he places his large, strong hands beneath my armpits and lifts. He's thinking that he can make me. I smell his Old Spice aftershave and breathe deeply in, letting my legs and body go slack but I am not heavy, even as dead-weight. He carries me to the bathroom, sets me on the closed toilet seat, and locks me in with a test. "You drive me wild," he says from behind the door he's holding shut, and this makes me smile.

This standoff makes it seem like he never left. His mistake, I relish, is that he's left me with my toothbrush and water pick. I begin my nightly routine and by measures feel calmer. When my teeth are clean, I pull the bath towels into the tub and make a bed there.

In the morning the house is quiet, and my period has come. I imagine my husband slumped against the door frame, sleeping. Or that maybe he's lying in our bed, and maybe that softness or the morning light will bring about some change of heart. He will wake up feeling refreshed and hopeful, and I can see him in my mind's eye, his dark hair stiff at odd morning angles. It strikes me then that this will be the end of us, this lack of child, that it was really the last thing that might have saved us.

I feel dirty with sleep in my eyes and dried blood between my legs, and I reach for the electric toothbrush and stand there for at least a half hour, until my gums begin to bleed too. This demon inside me, I think. This awful curse.

I take all my things, even the new water pick, and put them in the trash. I pour the prescription mouthwash down the drain. It was expensive, and it pains me to watch the last swill of it disappear. I try the door handle, and it gives, and he is there on the floor, bent over. It doesn't take much to wake him. "Look," I say. "Look what I've done. I did it myself." I feel swollen and proud, and for a moment like I will be able to conquer my obsession, like someone else has come in to relieve me, has taken over at the helm.

He sighs. He looks tired, not at all refreshed, and besides that, he looks past me, away from the trash can at the unopened pregnancy test. "Why can't you just take it?" he asks.

"Why can't you just trust me? Why can't you just believe in me?" I sound like I am going to cry, my voice high and too loud and cracking. I can't bring myself to tell him the truth, not right now, not while my toothbrush is in the trash, not while there is such a small distance between our bodies. He already looks defeated, and I see that I've already won this battle, that it's over.

"How can you just stop loving someone?" I say meanly, which is an accident. I am angry, I realize. Furious.

"You can't." He begins to cry in earnest, loud and ugly sobs. "I can't. But you're not well. Walking away is the best thing I can do for you." This last part is almost a whisper, and it doesn't make sense, it's illogical.

I think of enamel, how it is the hardest substance in the human body, all mineral and tissue. I think about how I am like this, a hard substance, sharp-edged. It's important, I think, to protect what protects you. He is waiting for me to say something, to plead, or to weep, but I find that I cannot even as I am devastated. I am wishing that I could crumple into his arms, but I know what will soothe me.

"You're so cold," he says, leaving again. "You're glacial. You're a desert."

Once he is gone I do the inevitable. I take off my wedding ring and throw it out the kitchen window. It will land somewhere in the rock garden where perhaps it belongs. While my husband drives away, already beginning his new life, I think about that diamond planet, so far away, and how he might have been more careful with his metaphors. I think about how that planet and its neutron star might have had all the right ingredients, the makings of something, but really it was just a failed little universe, isolated and far beyond reach.

Glass-Bottomed Bovine

Allison Barrett

I'm in the milk and the milk's in me!
— Maurice Sendak

My daughter's fingers poke through the crocheted
holes in her blanket. She probes shadows and wipes light on her hands.
Neighbors' voices
burble up through the floor. She's recently passed
through a body that was a place as far
as she knew. She heard voices there too. One day she'll skip the cracks
in the boardwalk, hunch as far away from the bathtub's drain
as possible, lest she risk another world.

When she sees a dandelion, she says *hot*. Gentle
pollen wafts by and wedges into my membranes
until I want to rub my face off. The woman downstairs
indicates with her hands what our leaky faucet
is doing to her ceiling— she appears to clutch generous buttocks.
Three miles away grazes a cow with a window
grafted into its side. I can see this as the next plastic surgery craze:
apertures that prove one is also beautiful on the inside—
deep, even. Pure!

I would teach my daughter to locate crows at night. To marry
a tree: bite its trunk and writhe in its branches, then run away
as often as you like. She'd teach me to punch holes through a tin
to sieve the night of stars, the evening gowns of sequins.
But I'm only guessing, since we can't see into one another.
Meanwhile, the walls hiss with water. We won't be dreaming
when we land at our neighbors' breakfast table
wearing our drywall suits. Surely they'd been expecting us.

The Catch

Allison Barrett

When the moon falls, it will not be slow
like a penny in syrup. No one will gentle
its descent, there will be no giant net, no birds
with pulleys in their beaks.

It won't fit your eye like a monocle then.
As it hurtles like a semi
to Earth, we'll have to acknowledge its true
heft, round as a dimpled rump. Remember
when your body began its bulge and shift?
How you tried to get away from yourself?

Pity the citizens gathered on dewy lawns
with arms outstretched—tender, stupid
gestures that will recommend them
to no one when even the oceans
have stopped reaching.

Frequently Asked Questions: 5

Camille T. Dungy

Do you have big plans for her first birthday?

Tomorrow this will all be over. She will take a step
        and the tide that fills the tide pools will come in.

The last crop of almonds in the world must begin as nothing
        but a thousand thousand miniscule blossoms.

I have loved every cell of her body from the time I could count them
        until now.

Why hurry her progress when each day is as gorgeous as the last?

She will take a step and the beekeeper will plant his hives in the orchard,
                walk away.

Field Trip

Camille T. Dungy

They hate this stuff, want them some chicken, she said, tossing bored yard dogs boneless breasts of chicken. We understood what she meant only when the crate had been opened and five de-beaked birds stopped flapping their fleshed and feathered carcasses around the yard, bodies assigned to one pile, heads to another. The dogs drooled, but by then the children's heads were mostly bowed or covered. Sharmaine pulled her little brother's body to her chest and maybe she was crying though with her I can never quite tell and Tyrone was sitting all of a sudden, crouching really, and biting his knee to hold back tears. *You can't do that*, we said, but of course it had already been done, and she couldn't see why not, she'd grown up here, and what was it we'd brought the kids to see? The sterile packages she'd send to market later? *In the old days birds fought back*, she said, assuming it was the speed of the dispatch that alarmed us. *I once gave up a goose got away seventy-one times, ran around this damn yard near all afternoon before Old Bo got a grip on him and lost an eye for his trouble. These de-beaked things, they have no fight*, she said, her hands still slick from tossing unwrapped, expired breasts to distract the dogs, a ruddy feather planted just above her lip. On her signal, Frankie and Will opened another crate and several necks were simply severed. Bo, one eye open, head square on his paws, kept the young ones in their corner. Those dogs, they licked each other's muzzles and their own.

Fish & Whistle

Rutherford Sullivan

I remember the Fourth of July when I was fourteen, being at summer camp in the Ozarks far from home, me and my best friend standing on the bank of the lake. The way the air sat heavy upon our small frames, sweat collecting on our brows and running down into our eyes, trees and earth seeping into our pores. How the water reflected the shapes and curves of the hills like stillborn copies of themselves. The other faceless boys and we were among them like we were all one body, tender-faced and boney and immaculate in the daylight.

The turtle someone caught in the shallows and how large and sinister it looked, bigger than my chest. The way it hissed and bit at our shins, watching a counselor kill it with a staff and hang it from a sapling at the water's edge. Cheering in harmony and how proudly the counselor smiled, his teeth crystalline and flawless. The way the turtle's neck stretched down from the rope like a serpent. Its bone torn and swinging from flesh alone. The length of firecrackers they wrapped around its shell, boys crowding around and girls turning away. Seeing the fuse spark then shorten. The turtle's insides rained down over us, chords of intestine and liver. *For America!* someone yelled. Everyone's glee from its ruin. Not feeling brave and not feeling tough and not feeling strong. My best friend smiling at me but just for a moment, blood freckling our faces. A counselor picking up a shard of organ from the red dirt and smearing the dark blood over his bare chest. *Men!* he yelled.

Running through the woods to the dock, the imperial pines reigning over our heads. Getting bamboo rods from the shed and casting our lines and watching our bait sink down into the velvet-green water. The postcard my best friend showed me that he had gotten from his mother, a picture of the Confederate monument from our hometown printed on the front. It read that she had gotten married without him and someone new would be there when he returned, someone he had never met. I did not tell him that things would be okay or that I was sorry or ask him if there was anything I could do. Standing in silence amongst the swarm and hum of the other kids and watching my line sway in the breeze that came off the water.

Another boy I did not know caught a fish and put a bottle rocket in its mouth and set it back into the lake. Feeling the tug on our lines almost simultaneously, reeling in our fish as their muscled bodies broke over the water's threshold. Holding them by their lower lips as they contorted their spines and placing our own bottle rockets down their open throats, setting them back. Watching them disappear into the darkness, the brief ghost of light coming from the bottom. The fish exploding in silence with the fragments of their bodies floating to the surface, most without jaws or underbellies. Everyone doing it. A symphony. *Fish don't have souls,* someone said. We laughed. Me and my best friend staring into the murk and watching the tiny explosions flicker like a constellation of stars hidden under some sacred blackness.

The day waned as we walked back to our cabin. Still sharing the blood of the turtle, dried and caked to our cheeks, and our hands smelling of gunpowder and shimmering from the remnants of scales between our fingers and under our fingernails. Low concussions off in the distance, the sky illuminating red and blue, and watching it glisten above our heads. The elegance of the lights fading into the blackness, dissolving away into the void above the water.

We came in and peeled off our clothes. The white shower room with its three showerheads, no curtains and no door. Black mold plastered to the walls and the bareness of our naked bodies as we washed and tried not looking down even though we all did. *We're all men here,* my counselor yelled in from the other room. Agreeing. We scrubbed ourselves raw and silver soft pink. Drying off and lying in my bunk and sweating through my cotton pillow case. My counselor reading of David and Solomon. Still smelling of fish and fireworks. Sleeping well.

The Place that Waits for You

Kristi Moos

Grizzly bears were once abundant in California. They roamed throughout the coast live oak woodlands of the San Francisco Bay Area. In 1827, soldiers in a boat came upon a grizzly swimming to Angel Island. The bear "approached the boat, intending to climb into it, when the soldiers fired four balls at close range, just as the bear was getting its claws upon the boat, and killed it stone dead."

—Tracy I. Storer and Lloyd P. Tevis, *California Grizzly*

Just across the water,
paradise:
groves of virgin oak,
fields of rabbit smut and deer rub
ready to be romped.

With salt-braided fur
and clawed oars,
you ferry over
to the place
that waits for you:

Sun-warmed shores
of brine-cured salmon,
grass-smeared mouse belly,
fifty pairs of cormorants
sailing overhead.

Yet closer,
you see a sliver of dry land:
a seaworthy river willow
heavy with good meat, steel,
and hot blood.

You will never shake off the bay
                    and its whalebone stink.
                              You will not see the four flares
          sink each hollering lung
into peace.

                    Your paws will fly up
          over the waves.
You will be an angel
          drifting
                    all the way to shore.

from *now, 1/3,* 6.1

Demosthenes Agrafiotis

the snow absorbs noises (memories)
confectioner's sugar on the bread and around the plate
shapes, contours
the pedestrians in the corners

the building admits nuns now
to die there

moonlit night, freezing hands
quickly to the kingdom, prefabs
                    unequal divinations

who got cured?
who stayed behind to keep track?
who might *Dirk Van Den Broek* be?
Who defies suicide?

computing the trams
counting shrouded faces
specialization

the cat stuck on the window pane
over an open notebook
for the window to become
a stage without a prompter

flame

he focused intently on the tight trousers
grant us–
let the decision come
dreams, proposals
the opportunity
boredom

soft snow
as the children return from the rivers
drink soups and beers
time creeps on the walls
Djemile? irritable like Chrysanthe

anxiety about oblique instruments
embalmed stags carried on the shoulders
sacrifice of freeze frames
and of impressions

SPECIALITEITEN.

—January 27-28, 1996
(Amsterdam-Maastricht)

Translated by John Sakkis and Angelos Sakkis

from *now, 1/3*, 6.2

Demosthenes Agrafiotis

stirrings, stirrings
how many sexes?

La betise humaine eternelle

rose
comes back with white hair
movable signs of deterioration
"ah, how life is!"

as we drive
        grandma demands respect
        writing proves vulnerable

bulletins

—February 4,1996
(Athens)

Translated by John Sakkis and Angelos Sakkis

Mosswood Park

John Sakkis

let me quickly seek the tracks if you can bind the bow and sleep it all off then take the train to Constantine, I promise that we will find our way whenever we can, it is better to avenge if you can, better to slip your way down the street than chew your house to pieces and as you know moths have flown into people's ears throughout history bearing the bloody cabinets you open when moving anywhere you thought you'd never be but it's only now that we have the means to remove them in the depths this day we're naming our children after our saints who are our fathers and mothers but only with patience along the peninsula when ears are technology and this all becomes rope-thin, figs are flowers and your good name will live on long after this weird patience bears our bloody wax men following their ears are shapely and extended towards the neighborhoods moving in and about this proximity of family as nowhere else seems to settle the stomach as much as organs identifying themselves at first impression

The Movie Quitters

Siamak Vossoughi

The movie was wonderful, beautiful, heartbreaking.

"The hell with this," my uncle said. "I'm tired of being moved to tears by American movies. When are they going to be moved to tears by Iranian movies? It's no good."

He wiped his eyes. "I've had it. I've had it with their joys and sorrows and their music in the background. It is too beautiful. I do not have the room inside myself any more. I have seen too much."

"It was a good movie," my aunt said.

"Of course it was a good movie. That's the whole problem. William," my uncle said to my cousin Niloufar's husband William "When are your parents coming to visit?"

"Three weeks."

"Okay. When your parents come to visit, we are going to watch a sad and beautiful Iranian movie. I am sorry. It has come to this. Look at me. I am crying. I am crying over an American movie. I am not going to feel good until I see an American man crying over an Iranian movie."

"What about an American woman crying?" my cousin said.

"That will help. But a man understands another man's tears."

"That is a man for you," my aunt said. "Even when there is something that you do not do as freely, you think that there is something special when you do it."

"I did not say that it is special. I said that I understand it."

"But the underlying point is that women cry too easily."

"I am not smart enough to have any underlying points. If I knew about underlying points, I would've noticed what all these American movies are doing to me."

"What?" I said.

"They are making me nostalgic for memories I don't even have. They are making me remember things I don't even know. 'Ah yes, good old America in the 1950s.' It is ridiculous. What the hell do I know about America in the 1950s?"

"Isn't that the point of a good movie?" my cousin said. "To make you feel like you are inside it?"

"Yes, of course," my uncle said. "That is why I am crying. But it is not a two-way street. It is not a free and open exchange. I am through. For my part, I am through. Until I see an American man or woman cry over an Iranian movie, I am done with them."

Over the next three weeks my uncle read seventeen books. He told me about them when I came to visit.

"Did you know that there are more sheep than people in New Zealand?" he said.

"Yes," I said.

"I have been sticking to it. No movies. I have been remembering myself."

"That's good," I said.

"Yes," he said. "Come on. Let's go to the video store. William's parents are coming tomorrow. We need to find a movie that is sad but not too sad. It shouldn't take our saddest movie to make them cry."

"I don't think there are any Iranian movies that are sad but not too sad."

We went to the Iranian video store in Bellevue. My uncle explained what he was looking for to Mr. Houshang, the owner.

"All movies are sad," Mr Houshang said. "American or Iranian. Do you know why?"

"No," we said.

"Because when we watch them, we see how hard we have been trying. Look at them. Look at how hard they have to work to make a movie. Look at how many people it takes. What is all that work for? It is to try to be us. Good God, we have been working hard."

He gave us a movie that he said was sad but not because of anybody young or beautiful dying.

"I think he is a wise man," I said when we left.

"Yes," my uncle said. "I was not prepared for that much wisdom. Maybe I have been thinking about this all wrong. I have been thinking of how much I have been giving of myself to American movies. I have not been thinking of what American movies have been giving me."

My uncle was quiet for a while.

"All right, all right," he said. "But is it a lot to ask for a two-way street? Is it a lot to say that I would like to see an American man cry as I have cried?"

"No," I said. "Or a woman."

"Or a woman," my uncle said.

The night that we watched the movie, I was trying very hard to not look at William's father and mother to see if an American man or woman would cry watching an Iranian movie. William's father did not seem like the kind of man who cried very often. He seemed like the kind of man who cried over a movie hardly ever. I thought my uncle was up against it. He was going to be reading books for a while.

The movie was wonderful and beautiful and heartbreaking. My uncle cried, and I did too. It was our country, and we missed it, and we didn't care what anybody else thought.

"The hell with it," my uncle said. "I am not watching any more Iranian movies. It is too sad."

It *was* too sad. I didn't like to think that there was a people just like us in every way except for everything about us that was from living in America and everything about them that was from living in Iran. It didn't make any sense. I understood why my uncle had decided to quit watching American movies. It was a lot just to be from one place and watch the movies from there.

"I wish I knew how you felt," William's father said.

"What do you mean?" my uncle said.

"I would like to know how it feels to feel a movie is too sad," William's father said. "I have watched movies that are sad, but the movie ends and I am back in the world."

"What is it like when you are there?" my uncle said.

"Where?"

"Back in the world."

"I don't know. It is the world. I have always been there."

"It is not the movie, it is the world," my uncle said to me that night after everybody had left. "It is like coming back from a trip and seeing where we live for the first time."

"Where do we live?"

"We live in America. But we also live everywhere we've ever been.

We might also live in places we've never been. I don't know. Sometimes I suspect that that is the case. But the movie touches those parts, those parts that have lived everywhere. It is a very lucky thing to have lived in more than one place, Hamid. It is sad too, but in this world, it is a very lucky thing."

I couldn't explain it, but I knew that he was right. I thought that maybe I should give up movies too if it meant understanding things like that.

Bees of Frankfurt Airport

Michael Sandler

Test it. A taste pure
as any in the Taunus or up the Main.
Pollution of an idea, that honey drawn
next door to runway fume and exhaust
would immure the heavy metals,
its stickiness trap
or snare as in a sewage treatment plant!
The heather and buckwheat spikes still erect
though dusted with residue,
the pollen pocketed
in swarms and ferried to the drawer of a box hive—
and yet the liquor's clear, like filtered light.

Waves of jet roar attuned
to a terminal's siren call,
vibrating glass honeycombed
in titanium struts above, a hum
of fast-food lines and luggage carts beneath,
though its enticements shimmer beyond the field
of view, reader boards flipping
Singapore, Tenerife, Marrakech, no ear cocooned
from where this is headed
even if tethered like a windsock to its pole—
the wax? A waning hypothesis:
its silence holds the missing slag.

Another day of takeoffs and landings
and gleanings unaccounted for—
collective knowledge unshared,
knowledge ciphered
in chemic code and response, helixed on an urge
to build more, fly farther.

As they transmute it to gold,
a muted presage of viscera lead-swollen,
a temple brought down,
and a dry wind riffling crusts
of amber strewn
inside a carcass jagged with spar and glass.

Stork

Rebecca Foust

Vows broken like bird bones. You spanned abyss intention
with flight, made that leap into glide

into not-faith. Or was it flat-spin oblivion that hurled you
towards Circe, her shining whetstone

honing the wishbone you'd left behind, the hope you'd
ever come home? You crash-landed

in shatter and grit, matted tuft and thirst. The years ground
down golden and slow, sand

in the mouth of a cove combed by waves. Now you are old,
and the sea withdraws her tide, gently terrible,

your foothold in quicksand, knee-deep in what once
was an isthmus. The neap tide

has passed with the autumn migration, leaving you mute;
even Christmas has forgotten your name.

A New Suit for Graduation:

Ivan Hobson

You're the first of us, my dad tells me
as he leans on the tailor's counter
unfolding a stack of twenty-dollar bills
worn and soiled as his swing-shift fingers;

as if he was my grandfather
leaning on his welding bench
sweating pipe at the shipyard before dawn;

as though he was my great-grandfather
leaning on his plow handle
while inches of Kansas blew away.

My Father's Heart

John Yearley

(Lights come up on an office. The door is almost closed. It is just after 7 p.m. Chris sits behind his desk. He leans back in his chair and stares at the ceiling. A knock is heard. Pause. Another knock. Brian tentatively enters. He holds a piece of paper.)

BRIAN: Sir? Do you need to look at this?

(Pause)

It's the latest draft. Of the letter.

(Chris looks at Brian. His face wears a quizzical expression.)

For the proposal?

But I just made the changes that everyone agreed on, so you didn't really need to…I mean, you should look at whatever you want, of course…

(Chris looks intently at Brian. Brian is extremely uncomfortable.)

Well, if we're going to make the last FedEx I guess we're going to have to go with what we got…

CHRIS: How old are you?

BRIAN: What?

CHRIS: How old are you?

BRIAN: I'll be twenty-six.

CHRIS: When?

BRIAN: Soon.

CHRIS: Do you have any tattoos?

BRIAN: Pardon?

CHRIS: Do you have any tattoos?

BRIAN: Why do you ask?

CHRIS: My son. He got a tattoo.

BRIAN: I didn't know you had a son.

CHRIS: I do. He got a tattoo.

BRIAN: What is it of?

CHRIS: I don't know that I can tell you that.

BRIAN: Oh, that's okay.

CHRIS: What I mean to say is, I don't know if I have the vocabulary, the descriptive powers, to do justice to the hideous fucking abortion that now decorates my son's left arm.

It's like this…head. Except it's got, I don't know, maybe ten eyes? And they're all shooting out of this head on these long, fibrous tendons. And there's this huge tongue exploding out of gigantic lips that comes to rest on a naked girl. She's masturbating, I think.

It's massive. Goes all the way from his elbow to his wrist. You can barely see any skin at all.

BRIAN: How old is he?

CHRIS: Sixteen.

BRIAN: That's illegal.

CHRIS: For all the good that does me now.

(Pause)

He was a mistake.

BRIAN: What?

CHRIS: My son. He was a mistake. I know you're not supposed to say that. Like it's a big taboo. But it doesn't mean anything. The moment they put that kid in your arms, and he looks up at you—and you're his daddy! You!—plans got nothing to with it anyway.

You know, I thought I would grow into fatherhood. Like over time his personality would form and I would love him for the person that he became. But the second I looked down at that wrinkled little face lying in the crook of my arm, the *instant* I saw him, all I could think was, "I would die for you."

BRIAN: That's nice.

CHRIS: Yeah. It was. But you know what isn't nice? My son now. Not so nice.

BRIAN: He's a troubled boy, sir?

CHRIS: "Troubled" would be one way to put it. "Asshole" would be another.

BRIAN: It's a difficult age.

CHRIS: I know. And I expected a lot. What I didn't expect was that he would turn out to be a total fucking douche bag.

You know, I actually hate him.

The other day I came home and he was dead drunk. He was passed out on my bed, his pants were around his ankles, his dick was hanging out, and this incredibly potent mixture of salsa and vomit was *everywhere*—all over my bed and on my pillows and in my carpet.

I thought about strangling him. I thought how good the bump of his Adam's apple would feel against my thumb as I squeezed, his eyes popping open as he gasps for breath…

BRIAN: I think I hear my phone…

CHRIS: He hates everyone! He thinks everything is stupid! The closest he gets to any kind of engagement with the world is this withering adolescent contempt. He gets no joy, as I far as I can tell, from anything except humiliation. Debasement seems to be the only thing that gives him any pleasure at all.

That and pissing me off.

(Chris leans back in his chair again. Pause. Brian has absolutely no idea what to do.)

You never answered my question.

BRIAN: What question?

CHRIS: A tattoo—do you have one?

(Pause)

BRIAN: I'd rather not say.

CHRIS: Jesus Christ! What is it?

BRIAN: Uh…well, it's kinda hard to explain.

CHRIS: Can I see it?

BRIAN: Uh…

CHRIS: It's not on your ass, is it?

BRIAN: No!

CHRIS: Well, can I see it?

I mean, if you didn't want anyone to see it, you probably shouldn't have etched it in permanent ink on your body. Am I right?

Come on!

BRIAN: Well, uh…

(Brian unbuttons the sleeve of his shirt. He pulls it back to reveal a small, discreet tattoo on his right forearm. Chris looks at the tattoo for several moments. He squints. He looks back at Brian.)

CHRIS: What is that?

BRIAN: It's an aortic valve.

CHRIS: A what?

BRIAN: An aortic valve. It's the valve in your heart that regulates the blood flow through your aorta. That's, like, the biggest chamber. Of your heart.

CHRIS: Okay.

BRIAN: My father was a heart surgeon.

CHRIS: Okay.

(Pause)

Surely you don't think that's a sufficient explanation.

BRIAN: Well, the thing is, he, uh…why is your son so mad at you?

CHRIS: What?

BRIAN: Well, he's acting out, right? I mean he jerks off in your bed, pukes, and then passes out. But not before spreading salsa on, like, *everything you own*. You don't have to be Freud to figure out he's probably kinda pissed at you.

I mean, it's none of my business. But you did actually kinda make it my business by telling me all that stuff, 'cause it's not like I asked or anything.

(Pause. Brian refers to the letter.)

I'm just going to send this off as is.

(Brian turns to go.)

CHRIS: Are you pissed at your father?

(Brian stops.)

BRIAN: My father's dead.

CHRIS: That doesn't answer the question.

(Brian laughs. He seems to give the question serious thought.)

BRIAN: No, I'm not pissed at him.

CHRIS: When did he die?

BRIAN: A year ago June.

CHRIS: I'm sorry.

BRIAN: Thank you.

CHRIS: What happened?

BRIAN: Heart attack.

CHRIS: Ironic.

BRIAN: I guess.

CHRIS: Well, I'm sorry.

BRIAN: Thank you.

CHRIS: How long have you had that tattoo?

BRIAN: Six months.

CHRIS: So you got it after your father died?

BRIAN: Yes.

CHRIS: Was it a tribute to him?

BRIAN: Sort of.

CHRIS: What do you mean sort of?

BRIAN: It's more like…a reminder.

CHRIS: Reminder of what?

(Brian says nothing. He looks very uncomfortable.)

Reminder of what?

BRIAN: Sir, do you not want to look at this? 'Cause if I'm going to make the 7:30 FedEx I've gotta go now.

(Pause)

CHRIS: To answer your earlier question, my son comes by his rage honestly.

His mother and I split when he was very young. He lived with her. A year ago I went to pick him up and found him cowering in a corner while she hurled jagged pieces of a broken ceramic lamp at him. He had this cut on his forehead. And she was screaming like…

He's lived with me since then.

Thing is, I knew when he was a baby that she was trouble and got the hell out. But I let him stay. I figured as long as I stayed in this stupid fucking place and handed her half my paycheck every week it was sacrifice enough.

But it wasn't. Not nearly enough.

I try to make it up to him now. I try to talk to him, take him places. He hates it.

BRIAN: I'm sure he appreciates the effort.

CHRIS: It would be hard to deduce that from his response.

BRIAN: *(laughing)* I bet!

CHRIS: And I try. I try to look in his eyes and see the kid, the kid that I know—I fucking know—is in there. And I can't. I just see my own frustration staring back at me.

And his disgust. His disgust at my helplessness.

And so now he's got this tattoo, this permanent fucking billboard telling the world that, despite all my sacrifice, I was a shitty father.

And he's right. He's absolutely right.

(Pause)

You can go. This is not your problem.

BRIAN: The tattoo. Your son's tattoo?

CHRIS: Yeah?

BRIAN: It's not about you.

CHRIS: He knows how much I hate tattoos.

BRIAN: But even if he did it to piss you off, it's about him. Not you.

He's not a reflection of you. Good or bad. The best you can do is just …love him. And try to…

CHRIS: Try to what?

(Pause. Chris points at Brian's arm.)

Hey, let me ask you something—what is that? Forgive me for saying so, you don't really seem like the tattoo type.

(Brian laughs.)

Seriously, why do you have that?

(Pause)

BRIAN: You have to understand, my father was a stern man. I

mean, I'm sure that he loved us and all, but it was kinda hard to tell.

Well, one year my class had this thing where your parents come in and talk about their jobs. So I asked my dad if he would come in, and he said yes.

See, my father and I didn't really ever talk. I think he thought I was kind of an idiot, 'cause I was so quiet. So before he came to class, I went through his library. Read all about the heart.

His presentation was really cool. He brought this cow's heart and dissected it in front of the class. And every time he was about to point something out, I would raise my hand, shout out what it was. Like, if it had been a test, I would have gotten a 100. I was on!

I assumed he would be proud of me, think maybe he didn't raise such a dipshit after all. But then he pointed at something in the heart and he turned towards me. Faced me full-on and looked me right in the eye. And the expression on his face...

You know, I don't think my father looked me in the eye very much. Because when he did...it was like being slapped.

I didn't say another word. The rest of the period I just looked at that heart on the table. The way it lie there, all grey and lifeless. And I thought, "That's your father's heart. And that's what he feels about you."

CHRIS: I very seriously doubt that.

BRIAN: Yeah.

(Pause)

So, anyway, the part he was pointing at when he glared at me was the aortic valve.

CHRIS: Oh.

BRIAN: Yeah. And when he died I found out that that was actually the part of his heart that malfunctioned. It had become calcified. Didn't allow enough blood into his heart.

(Brian pulls up his sleeve, shows the tattoo to Chris. Chris takes Brian's arm in his hand.)

See, if you look at it closely, the valve is open all the way. I made sure they drew it like that.

I actually had somebody tell me once that that could be dangerous, too. Like if the valve was too open it could flood your heart and kill you. But I figure everybody's gotta die. That wouldn't be such a bad way to go.

(Chris releases Brian's arm. He steps back, breathes deeply, looks at the ground. Chris awkwardly rolls down his sleeve.)

Anyway, I'll go send this off.

CHRIS: That's okay, I'll take it.

BRIAN: Oh, you don't have to do that.

CHRIS: No, I want to.

(Brian hands the paper to Chris.)

It's late. You should go home.

BRIAN: Okay.

CHRIS: Thanks for staying late.

BRIAN: No problem.

CHRIS: It's nice.

BRIAN: Pardon?

CHRIS: Your tattoo. It's…nice.

BRIAN: Oh. Thank you.

(Pause)

You have a good night, sir.

CHRIS: Thanks. You, too.

(Brian walks to the doorway.)

BRIAN: You want this open or closed?

CHRIS: Open. Please.

(Brian exits. Lights fade to black. End of play.)

The Test

Ace Boggess

into a cup I pour my admission of innocence
temporal evidence in the body's court

another day passes a month a year &
suddenly half a decade devoted to the Grail

how it tests one's purity
despite the bloody errantry of past crusades

the heat strip lights up like Mars in transit
as black bars in pairs appear like a prison made from night

all because I gave myself release
expressed my nature in line art to the critic cup

it tells me not that I can do no wrong
but that wrongs I've done are done with

for at least this pause this sighing hallelujah
I walk without daggers in my eyes

without regrets without new ones anyhow
this golden mead this liquor of sobriety

Chronic Lymphocytic Leukemia

Gail Rudd Entrekin

When the monster grabbed him up, tossed him back
into its mouth, we had been swimming along holding hands
and I didn't let go, flew up dripping and dropped beside him
into the dark and foreign place where there were others
dimly swimming for their lives and there were teeth that grazed
our skins now and then as we lay very still, our hope ballooning,
rising up into the sinuses of the creature intermingled
with our fear so that both rose equally and were, we prayed,
equally compelling, but the truth, we knew, was that the beast
was dumb and barely knew we were there.
Every day
it tested its spikes against our naked fragile bodies,
some days teasing us by tipping forward, almost letting
us roll out into the frothy sea, but most days we lay still,
read medical books, listened to the messages of friends
sending love and encouragement from far away places
where life went on in warm kitchens and the linens
were clean and dry.
Finally, the thing decided not to decide,
let us wash out with the tide. We are swimming again
and the ocean is very blue. But there is a fin moving
beside us on the horizon and though it disappears
from time to time in the bright sun
at dusk it is always there
circling.

a small lapse into imperfection

Linda King

myth balances darker truths
like soft weather from some Greek tragedy
where everything returns through language

every story ever written concerns you
a balance sheet of verbs   adjectives at the door
thread of facts alive with verdicts
everyone texting their own story

there is more naming to come
this is what happens in trickery
you must recite random lists of contradictions
endure hours and hours of questions
in rooms of sad translation

your prayers are simple
the small parts of each day

this map becomes the dream
helps you get used to the idea of evolution
cardboard boxes filled with bones

all that walking barefoot
toward various forms of warmth

from *January Yes*

MRB Chelko

The man played. Saxophone. In midnight Penn Station. Slow. You and I stopped speaking. Gave him no money. Neither did we understand. How the song could give voice to a group of strangers. How we rode home. A note. Completely. Without time or reason. Space or wings. We knew only. It was not work. That music. Not New York shrinking.

Artists' Biographies

Gilda Davidian (cover artist) is a photographer living and working in Los Angeles. She graduated from CalArts in 2006 and is currently an MFA candidate at the Milton Avery School of Arts at Bard College. More of her photographs can be seen at gildadavidian.com.

Mitchell Maher is concerned with the problems of home, primarily. Patterns of the house—the protection of the nook, invisibility in the attic, fear in the basement, the grace of a good hallway. Maher studied at the Speos Institute Photographique in Paris and at Lux Academy of Visual Arts in Los Angeles.

Sean Mikula lives and works in San Francisco, after spending his first twenty six years in Buffalo, New York. He'd always rather take a picture than be in it, and doesn't understand why people always seem to have their phones in the bathroom.

Untitled #1
Mitchell Maher

Untitled #2
Mitchell Maher

Untitled #3
Mitchell Maher

Untitled #4
Mitchell Maher

Jetlag *Sean Mikula*

I need better excuses *Sean Mikula*

I'm only like this when you're around *Sean Mikula*

This is nice, because it's supposed to be *Sean Mikula*

For Stacy, 1962-2012

Maxine Chernoff, Chair of Creative Writing

Stacy Doris exceeded all ready definitions and illustrated a generosity and ferocity of living and invention that I can only call genius. As my faculty member for a decade, Stacy purveyed great kindness to her students: sheer and utter brilliance of invention, an openness to poetry and its investigative methods that transformed the genre into gifts new and luminously transmutable by her insight and humanity...Whether it was vocal poetry, the poetics of listening, the craft of translation, or MFA Poetry Workshop, every semester Stacy offered pure innovation, something discrete and singly prepared for the group alone, never repeated, lovingly shared.

Her poetry escaped categorization. From her heady catalogues to intimate and tender love poems to complex parodies, Stacy's rich engagement with language is legendary and head-spinning for its virtuosity. She refused to be stuck in a single position or bored or to bore her reader. Her poetics of engagement and challenge, to make it new not only project to project but word to word, appears on every page.

—March 21, 2012

From *Knot*, ii.XIV

Stacy Doris

Achievement's model, same as pornography's, its equal, is the picnic:
Ornament and emblem of gratuitous though enforced consumption,
Tableau or charade, still-life, nausea of false abundance. Delight or any
Triumph's just evacuation, an airing for better housekeeping's benefit,
Working order rinsed and spit out: enshrined. To let go, hypnotic, beating,
To admit any moment as death for once makes it never too late. Then
Enjoying exceeds sensation and anyone learns that you're cut off from
Your feelings. They change. Since faith equivocates, professed, circulatory,
Thus laced with doubt, prohibition's release. Belief's agreement to loss,
So anyone sinks . Sound, a spiral, implies joy's centripetal, throwing mass
To concentrate. Somebody's an impression, left to fend, efferent where
Pooling bears, where waves refer to nerves.

In Memoriam

Kate Warne

The most ancient sculpture is a tiny Venus
her voluptous fractured figure
carved from mammoth ivory
and seeming everything
bigger than her two inches high

Stacy died yesterday
after poems, after strong
I picture her long clever face as I walk home

    Man in a suit says
Give me a smile girl   (come on—
up on your hind legs like a poodle)
drops the smirk when I don't
Honey becomes *Bitch!*

The categories can shift:
the tree can speak
the girl can grow a horn
Some sort of beauty is as good as healing

Stacy died yesterday

I think of the flute
found near Venus in her cave
imagine some knowing woman
drawing music from a vulture's wing bone
while the artist works
while the horses

Art can accept us or refuse us
This tune has traveled forty thousand years

On Validation

Michelle Carter

Part I: What We Want

Wake well-rested. Grains, fruit, wheat toast, no butter. Floss with confidence. Feel good about yourself and others will feel good about you.

The phone rings, the new email tone sounds, the Google Alert notification pops. The energy of the world rushes through the ether to you and you receive.

The coveted award. The lucrative grant. The blog rave. The review to die for. The top of the top ten list (alphabetical, but still). And with each, a flattering photo!

Has it happened? In this moment? Yes. Now.

You have arrived.

◊

The greater the success, the closer it verges upon failure.—Robert Bresson

◊

A good friend called yesterday, elated over a rave review of his play. "She has given me my life," he said of the critic.

◊

I don't trust people until I know what they love. If they cannot admit to what they love, or in fact love nothing, I cannot take even their smartest criticisms seriously.—Stephen Dunn

◊

Part II: What We Get

It's a quiet joy, arrival. A quiet thrill. You once were "I will be" but suddenly, now: "I am." I am *good.*

The moment stretches. Becomes another moment. What is this feeling? A surge of—what? Fear? *Fear of disappearing?*

How long has it been since you wrote the award-winning, blog-celebrated play? You have ideas for another. Pages of notes. You are between projects, that's all.

Every second, somewhere, an *is* is silently becoming a *was.*

What now? Where to turn?

Facebook.

Awards have three things to offer: cash, confidence, and bric-a-brac... The confidence-boosters have a temporary strengthening effect but, like good reviews, are dangerous: they lead the recipient to overestimate himself, and make him vulnerable to the disappointments which inevitably follow.
—Stephen Sondheim

9:30 a.m.: A great day to write. You will write. Why shouldn't you?

10:15 a.m.: This stuff is ridiculous. Bland. Slack. No energy, no tension, no subtext, no pressure. Whatever gave you the idea that you could write dialogue?

11:05 a.m.: Some inspiration—yes. Reread Churchill's *Far Away.* Dialogue with tension, subtext, pressure, and so forth.

12:30 p.m.: It's hopeless. You could never write dialogue that begins to approach the energy, tension, subtext, and so forth of Caryl Churchill's. You could never write a play that begins to approach the genius of *Far Away.*

2:25 p.m.: Remember how good _________ said you were at that thing you do? And that other thing you do? Do those things. Do those things a lot.

4:10 p.m.: Yes. School the people. Open their eyes. Tell them true things about being alive in diction so accurate, syntax so seductive, sentences so beguiling, rhythms so stirring that no one could doubt your mojo, your chops, your unmistakable badassness. They will hear your words and know…what do you want them to know? *That you are really good at this.* Isn't that the best any writer could hope for?

Isn't it?

◊

Part III: What We Do

Post the links on Facebook: the awards, the reviews, the blogs, the top ten lists.

I am honored and, above all, humbled.

What about friends who aren't on Facebook? Send an email blast. What of the colleagues of acquaintances who have kind of heard of you a little? Ask friends to post your website link to their Google+ circles.

The "Like" buttons click. The congratulations cascade. You are so well-liked that no one even pauses to wonder: *What is this behavior evidence of? An absence of self-regard, or an excess of it?*

"I am" becomes *I am seen.* The Recording Angel has you in his embrace.

But what has he written?

◊

An acquaintance, a playwright, attends every performance of her own play. As each performance ends, she waits in the shadows of a bottleneck through which each audience member must pass to exit. She has made note of everyone she knows in the house and when each approaches the exit, she sets upon him like Cato ambushing Inspector Clouseau.

What do you think?

What do I think? You wonder what you're being asked to respond to: the performance about which you're currently not feeling analytical, absorbed as you are in searching your pockets for your keys? Or the living, breathing spectacle of need before you, hoping for a benediction?

The playwright's hunger for validation becomes a force field between you and the work you've just seen. Tomorrow you'll try to conjure the experience of the play in your mind, but you won't be able to find your way back to it.

◊

A photograph must have room in it for entrance by outsiders, so that the photographer himself or herself hasn't built a structure that keeps you out, but instead has left some crack that allows you the freedom to enter. He or she hasn't held on too tightly. I heard a quote from Peter Mathiessen, who said that when you climb a mountain the first rule is "Don't cling.'" You have to climb a mountain free, as if you're just taking a walk on the beach. And I think if a photograph is made by a photographer who is trying to give you a message, you get that message but you don't have a real experience.—Joel Meyerowitz

◊

What other people think of me is none of my business.—Dorothy Parker

◊

Years ago an editor from Doubleday asked me to submit a story for an anthology. A close friend of mine was also a friend of this editor and offered to turn in my story for me. Days later he told me that the editor had accepted a story of his, and rejected mine.

Weeks later the phone woke me: it was the editor hoping to persuade me to submit a story for the book. The editor said my friend had told her I didn't want to contribute anything. Might I reconsider?

◊

Characters in a play are all in the dark. And in the end, they're all not guilty.—Alan Bennett

◊

Hundreds of artists submitted work for a New York gallery show in 1955. Robert Rauschenberg's submissions were chosen; the work of his friends was not.

Rauschenberg couldn't decide whether to go ahead with the show. He was happy for the chance to exhibit his work but unwilling to seem to have done so by besting his friends.

His solution: he exhibited a large "Combine," a collage of his own work and the work of his friends who'd been rejected.

◊

Don't enter awards competitions. Just don't. It's not good for you.—Bruce Mau

◊

When I was an undergraduate, my favorite professor agreed to do an independent study with me on the novels of Muriel Spark, a writer we both loved. I was very nervous. I'd only just changed my major to English and I had no idea how to talk about books.

The subject of our first meeting was *The Prime of Miss Jean Brodie*. In the course of my stumbling commentary I attacked Jean Brodie's character, calling her a Nazi. The next time I saw the professor he seemed cool, aloof. I asked if everything was all right. His reserve cracked and he snapped, with disappointment and genuine anger: "I will never forgive you for what you said about Jean Brodie."

A flash of shame, and then: the revelation, thrilling. *Jean Brodie matters. Muriel Spark matters. Books matter. Art matters.*

He forgave me in time.

◊

You owe it to students not to praise them. With praise you are passing up an opportunity to help them see what the goal is, to see it intellectually and to perceive it instinctively. They realize that if I give them praise it's a way of

not engaging them with analysis. They come to see praise as a shortcut. They find it unserious.—Jane Smiley

◊

I once took a demanding workshop where I was the only writer among a gifted group of dancers, actors, and directors. The workshop had a physically rigorous component. I'd had no movement training to speak of and I was the oldest person in the group. I suppose I expected to be cut a little slack.

In one exercise, we were taught a series of physical poses that were to be copied precisely and held with great stillness. Once the postures were learned one of the teachers slapped a bamboo stick to the floor: with each slap we were to shift, with catlike grace, from one posture to another. After a time I began to think: *I'm getting the hang of this. I think I've got it.*

The leader fell silent. She rose from the floor and crossed the stage to where I stood holding my pose.

Calmly and without inflection she said: "And you, you have failed. And everyone can see it."

You can't see yourself, nor can you see your work in the context of a practice to which I have devoted my life. I see you, your work, and what's at stake. You didn't come here to be comforted.

No. I had not.

◊

No artist is pleased. There is no satisfaction whatever at any time. There is only a queer, divine dissatisfaction, a blessed unrest that keeps us marching and makes us more alive than others.—Martha Graham

◊

I was sitting in the house for a performance of a play of mine at the New York Summer Play Festival. As the performance progressed, a large man next to me laughed, snored, laughed, snored, etc., in cyclic eruptions.

When the play was over the man applauded, turned to me, and said, "Who would *write* this play?"

Gulp. "I did."

He laughed again. "My subscribers would *hate* this play!"

He handed me his card: he was one of the best-known artistic directors in America. He said some nice things about the play and told me why he could never produce it. In that lovely, light moment, he released each of us from the pressure of our roles. The playwright: *I should impress this man somehow.* The artistic director: *Better tell a charming story so I can slip away without getting into what I think of her play.* He freed us of that mutually belittling ritual.

We talked about other plays in the festival. I made recommendations, he made recommendations. He hugged me goodbye.

i require a miracle. i require the humility and faith to allow it to happen. an army of a thousand cannot help me. it's down to the creative spirit of the universe and me. kicking and screaming.—Stephen Adly Guirgis, Facebook post

The Labyrinth production of *Our Lady of 121st Street*, fifth row, my second time. Next to me, a talkative lady who'd been brought to the play by her daughter. The lady was visiting New York from a small town in rural Kansas. She'd never seen a play before and she was very, very excited. Her daughter worked for a publishing house, and it was clear that her mother embarrassed her terribly.

Let's see: a man with no pants, a stolen corpse, a raped and murdered child, infidelity, drugs, a dead alcoholic nun, a lot of four-letter words, and a whole lot of shouting. The lady from Kansas's first play. How would she hold up?

God, how she laughed. Those whole-body, rocking-forward-and-back in your seat convulsing belly laughs. Foul-mouthed nasty Norca?

Hilarious. Poor Sonya gets socked in the mouth? Funniest thing ever. And the climactic scene where Inez tells Rooftop that he took her secret garden and dropped a fuckin' atomic bomb on it and now it's just scorched earth and ashes? Tears streamed down the lady's face. Inez's heart was broken, and so was hers. When the play was over, she could hardly stand.

This woman didn't want to be seen, or flattered, or reassured. The playwright didn't want to be seen or flattered or reassured, nor did the actors, nor the director, nor the designers, or anyone else in the building.

The world rushed through the performance to the lady from Kansas and back to the play and the artists and back to the lady from Kansas as each was being made more alive.

◊

As I begin to understand and respect it, the ritual of theater involves a transference of sensual life energy from one group of people to another.—R. G. Davis

◊

Day after day we wake again to find the world still here, waiting for us as we play out our own small dramas with their small triumphs and terrible heartbreaks. And then, remarkably, astonishingly, just here just ends. For me that is the mystery. No amount of explanation, be it a 'Theory of Everything' or a religious theology, will reduce the power of its experience. The primitive quality of feeling, the presence of life and its luminosity, is the mystery and I am damn thankful for it.—Adam Frank

◊

PART IV: What Everyone Is

Dust. Molecules. Jerks of infinity. We'd burst if we had the courage.

—Richard D'Elia
San Francisco State MFA
Facebook post

Interview with Michelle Carter

Kelly McNerney

Sadly, Michelle Carter finds it validating to tell you that her plays have received the Susan Glaspell Award, Backstage Garland Awards, the PEN West Award, and the PEN USA Literary Award in Drama. Her work has been produced and developed at theaters in San Francisco, Los Angeles, New York, Florida, Washington, New Jersey, and London, where she held a residency at the Donmar Theatre. She'll soon return to London to continue work on DREAMSPIEL: A Ukulele Opera, a collaboration with The Ukulele Orchestra of Great Britain. She has published short stories in many journals and anthologies as well as a novel with Penguin Books.

◇

14H: Before we talk about "On Validation," I was hoping I could pick your brain about your history with *Fourteen Hills*. What motivated you to start the journal? Did you have a certain vision for what you hoped the journal would be? What were the early trials and tribulations? How have you seen the journal change over the years?

MC: Confession: I am not the founder of *Fourteen Hills*. Matthew Davison, Faculty Advisor for *Fourteen Hills*, has referred to me as the founder in various circumstances and I swear I used to correct him. I have a feeling I stopped correcting him.

The founder of *Fourteen Hills* is the poet, memoirist, and cookbook and textbook author Frances Mayes. *Fourteen Hills* was Frances's idea.

Frances Mayes secured the funding. The founder of the feast was Frances Mayes. I took the magazine over soon thereafter, but I most certainly did not start it. And at this point, Matthew has been in charge longer than I ever was and has brought exciting dynamism and creativity to the enterprise.

I hope I've made that clear that it was Frances Mayes who founded *Fourteen Hills*. I hope Matthew keeps telling people it was me.

14H: Sufficiently clear I think! I have heard another rumor that you were once primarily a fiction writer. How did you make the transition into playwriting?

MC: I started writing plays as the result of a head injury. I got knocked in the head in a bad car accident and woke up bloody, on a stretcher, blanketed in the shattered windshield. As days passed I realized that I couldn't exactly read. I could "read" a word, then another word, then a phrase, then a sentence. What I couldn't do was put sentences and paragraphs together to create cumulative meaning. I didn't teach for a year and a half. I remember coming to the student awards reading with a weird mask over my face after surgery on my nose. "I'm Michelle Carter, but you can call me 'Crash,'" I told the audience. I thought this would be hilarious. It wasn't.

When it got through my head that returning to my 400+-page novel draft and 300+-page textbook draft might not be imminent, my post-accident survivor's high vaporized. I couldn't teach, I couldn't write—I felt like a thing whose sole function and purpose was to tend itself. I went to music and theater performances eager for revelation, looking for clues. I remember watching a Nilo Cruz play at the Magic Theatre and realizing that tears were streaming down my face. What I was discovering was that language you take in as sound and image—through your eyes and ears—lands in a different part of your brain from text you take off the page. Plays, I thought: maybe I could do this.

Over time I was able to read again, though the way I process meaning from written text has changed. I don't think I could explain it in words.

14H: I think that discovering "that language you take in as sound and image" is processed differently by the brain might do a pretty decent job. Just as a side note: I'm not going to call you "Crash" either. Though it seems healthy that you managed to have a sense of humor about the whole thing. Can you say anything about how fiction writing has helped or informed your playwriting?

MC: I thought the transition from fiction writing to playwriting would be a lot more seamless than it was. That particular transition requires letting go of a lot of things—an interest in narrative, back-story, connective tissue, nice sentences, "good writing." You have to learn to leave things out, to leave important things unarticulated so the audience can have an experience of them. I think poets tend to move into playwriting more naturally than fiction writers do.

14H: Do you have any advice for writers who want to experiment across genres but might feel intimidated or unqualified because it isn't "their" genre?

MC: One of the things I love about the program at San Francisco State is that students aren't locked into their genres of admission. There are so many great reasons to experiment outside your home genre. You don't know what you might discover when you're outside your comfort zone, leaving your old tricks behind. You enter a new genre with a mindset of experimentation. Taking risks. Nothing to prove. You don't know how your work in your home genre might be stretched or deepened by the journey outside it.

14H: When I went to see your play *Patience Worth* late last year, we talked a little about the general trend of shrinking audiences, and support for literary events, most specifically for plays. What can we do, as a part of the literary community in San Francisco, to revamp support for dramatic arts, get more people going to the theater?

MC: I wish I knew. Everyone wants to get younger people to the theater. Everyone wants to attract more diverse audiences. Part of the problem is the surfeit of white upper-middle-class, tasteful-living-room plays that draw white upper-middle-class people with tasteful living rooms. Also: theater is expensive. Also: a lot of theater is boring. Also: a lot of plays are like episodes of TV shows and you can watch TV at home. It's complicated I guess. There was a survey a few years back that asked people to list the reasons why they don't go to the theater, and the number one response was that they didn't know what they were supposed to wear.

14H. Well. Makes you wonder what the number two response was. In "On Validation," you mentioned taking part in a theatre workshop with other dancers, actors, and directors. Have you acted or directed? Were you at one time interested, or do you remain interested, in exploring other roles in theatre?

MC: After my accident I was eager to try to write plays, and though I'd loved theater all my life, I'd had no formal theater education beyond acting in plays in high school and college. So I spent several years over the past decade immersing myself in theater training outside the academy. I did summer workshops with Anne Bogart's SITI Company, Ruth Maleczech of Mabou Mines, Maria Irene Fornes, others. I also tagged along on some rehearsal and development processes led by artists I had huge respect for, like the dance/theater choreographer/artist/writer Joe Goode. And I also found ways to get myself to New York and London as often as possible.

Since theater isn't just words on a page, it's urgent that playwrights expose themselves to the craft and practice of actors, directors, designers, stage managers, all of it. The attitude of apprenticeship should never end.

14H: Lawrence Eilenberg once said, "Michelle Carter is one of the few contemporary American playwrights who is able to express the public and private with equal commitment." "On Validation" is a piece that I really think strikes that balance of exploring the public and the personal in such intriguing ways. One thing I keep coming back to about this piece is its intense honesty about insecurity, the need we have as writers for confirmation from others, juxtaposed and explored through Facebook posts, anecdotes, and conversations with other writers. Social media and the Internet are crazy phenomena, and also very concrete realities. Pervasive, for lack of a better word—particularly in the ways they relate to promotion of literary work. They make our private lives public to a certain extent, right? How much "reflecting" on social media, or how it relates to this idea of validation, played into the writing of this essay?

MC: I have the same love/hate relationship with social media that I expect most people do. There's much to love about Facebook. More than anything else I'm grateful for the opportunity to stay in touch with former students and with actors I've worked with outside the Bay Area. But I find myself having complicated feelings about how we use the Internet to make ourselves feel talented, special, worthy, validated. At best, I don't think it works so well; at worst, I fear, it's just not good for us.

I've been alive long enough to remember not only a world without social media, but a world without the Internet—without email. If you wrote a book, you'd collect the reviews on newsprint, and your agent would mail you clippings from outside your area. If a play of yours were being produced, people outside your immediate circle would find out when the theater sent out its season announcement. If you wrote something and it was to be published or performed or in some way celebrated, you'd tell your friends. You wouldn't take out an ad in a newspaper to announce that you were a semifinalist in the *Prairie Schooner* short fiction contest. That would have struck people as weird—and kind of pathetic.

I expect that many of us scroll through Facebook in a mildly self-loathing frame of mind. There's always something else we think we should be doing so we tell ourselves we'll just scroll for a few minutes, then shut Facebook down and get cracking on something important. I suspect that while on Facebook a person's self-esteem is inversely proportionate to the length of time he has spent on the site that day. So a Facebook post that feels to the poster like "sharing good news!" can hit the person who's feeling like a loser for blowing the afternoon online as shameless self-promotion. In that case, the poster isn't evoking sincere, unbridled admiration in the breasts of his Facebook friends—something quite the opposite. And even if he had impressed all comers: what would that really, truly do for him?

I wrote "On Validation" in the hopes of raising questions about our need, as artists, to feel worthy, to feel respected, to feel seen, heard, valued. To feel as if we have arrived. Is it possible to come into possession of a belief in ourselves and our work? And, if not, can't we just make art without it?

14H: Interesting questions to think about. I mean, in one sense, you want people to connect to your work, right? If you aren't reaching people on a certain level, engaging in "transference of sensual life energy from one group of people to another," then your work is not doing its job. So you want that confirmation from folks—that there is in fact some sort of transference taking place. But where, thereafter, does it become about our egos? What does "impressing" people have to do with our work or with the objectives of art? Hard stuff to tease apart.

You quote Jane Smiley (a former teacher at Iowa) in this essay, and your last quote is from a student here at San Francisco State in the MFA program. I have never had the pleasure of taking a workshop with you, but I am curious if you organize and structure your workshops like Smiley suggests we should, by withholding praise and engaging your students in a more analytic engagement. Is there a lot of resistance to this approach? To a certain extent our first, default, knee-jerk reactions in workshops are to say something "nice" or positive about a piece. "I like this" or "I like that," and we see that as being supportive. How much do you feel like you have to justify why a workshop would be run in this fashion, why praising work might not be beneficial or useful to writers?

MC: Jane Smiley talks about her method in an interview that I often share in the Teaching Creative Writing class. Based on conversations I've had with the excellent students that have taken that class, I think it's easy to misinterpret Smiley's intentions. I don't think that by saying "no praise" she's telling us that she and her workshop students aren't allowed to say positive or supportive things. I think she just doesn't allow students or herself to get away with pat, evaluative declarations, i.e. lazy judgments, positive or negative, that don't explore, inquire, or illuminate.

A well-intentioned workshop member might say of a piece: "I love the writing." This feedback gives the writer nothing to use to explore, develop, or even understand this draft of her work, nothing with which to re-engage it in revision. Moreover, the responder has given himself nothing intellectually or creatively or emotionally stimulating to do: he's trying to make somebody, and himself, feel good, and it will probably work. Sometimes if a teacher presses for more specific feedback you get something like: "I love the scene with the mother at the truck stop." That's nice: how might this responder go on to inquire of that scene? How might he give the writer insight into what she's done that effectively serves the story's intentions?

Imagine how a workshop responder who loves the writing or who loves the scene with the mother at the truck stop might make himself work harder. He might 1) begin by naming the elements that "work for him" as precisely as he can, and then 2) talk about how those elements function to serve the intentions of the story. Not "this works for me" but "this is how this works." The writer would then have the opportunity to hear active, concrete analysis of elements that are functioning effectively in her piece. Not unexamined reaction, but inquiry. And the workshop responder has had—to rob Smiley's phrase—the pleasure of analysis.

Not that writing that we love always surrenders to analysis. But a useful workshop discussion is less likely to be stimulated by "I love the writing" than by a focused, generous identification of particular elements that hold power: "I keep thinking about the moment on page ten where the old lady sings. It moved me and I don't know why. Let me read it out loud."

The process Jane Smiley is describing is positive, supportive, and stimulating. Much more so than lazy praise, which might make the writer glow for the rest of the day but isn't much for her to be paying tuition for.

14H: True. It seems that being asked to articulate in these inquisitive ways benefits not just the particular writer being workshopped at that moment (as they receive useful, constructive feedback on their work) but those being asked to respond, as well. I think it changes our level of awareness about technique and craft, and heightens our understanding of how plays or stories or poems actually function—and gives us ways to talk about that.

Thank you so much for continuing to share that conscientiousness and guidance with *Fourteen Hills*.

Nobody Moves, Nobody Gets Hurt

Lauren Waterman

When Chris got out of the cab on Avenue A, I didn't slide over.

I'd been sitting in the middle, squished between him and his boss. I always ride in the middle of the backseat because, if I can't see out the windshield, I get carsick. It's especially tough in taxicabs—staring around stickers and scratches in the bulletproof Plexiglas—but I'm usually okay if I stay centered.

Chris turned around and leaned back through the open door to press a kiss into my cheek, taking my right hand in his to deliver, overly solemnly, his half of some old secret handshake. "I'll call you tomorrow, tigerrrrr," he said, rolling the *r* into my ear, his tongue close enough to tickle. Then he straightened up, slammed the door shut, and started towards his building. The Boss and I sat there, still, until the driver's profile appeared in my little plastic porthole and I realized that neither of us had given him the next address.

"Eldridge and Houston, please," I said, without bothering to consult the bespectacled stranger seated beside me. No matter where The Boss lived, I figured, my place was on the way, and I was getting dropped off first.

Chris hadn't asked me to the party as his date; he never does. Instead, he called to see if I was up to serving as his "wingman," a by then totally ceremonial title that we clung to despite its having been besmirched by a dozen dumb beer ads in the years since we thought we invented it.

That was back when we first moved to the city after college, after I'd broken up with his best friend and he'd ended a drama-filled relationship with a girl I'd never really cared for. "Perhaps," he'd hazarded, one not-so-happy hour, "we could be of assistance to each other in lining up prospects?" The idea, as he explained it, was that we'd go out together, and if he saw a quote-unquote *lady* that he liked the looks of, I'd be the one to strike up a conversation, get her comfortable, and then he'd move in. And of course, he said, vice versa.

But it turned out to be a truly terrible plan. We spent entire evenings at bars talking only to each other, thereby effectively eliminating any chance that anyone attractive might actually make it easy by approaching either of us. And the few times that we *did* attempt to take action, we quickly discovered the scheme's fatal flaw: People—well, straight people, which is the sort we're looking for—are in fact far more interested in being hit on, however awkwardly, by a member of the opposite sex than in having someone of the same gender sidle up with a weird non-line about sports, for example, or shoes.

So when we got to his co-worker's cavernous loft, which was wide-open and under-furnished and featured, in one corner, a large, new-looking flat-screen TV stacked atop an even larger '90s-era model—we pretty much stuck together. We tossed our coats on a messy pile by the door and set off in search of alcohol.

◊

Two hours later, we were sitting side-by-side on a couch, drinking lukewarm Budweisers and watching, transfixed, while four of Chris's colleagues struggled to operate an enormous vintage stereo system. Music had been emanating intermittently from the waist-high, wood-cloaked speakers all night, but the thing had quit working entirely—quite possibly in protest—a few minutes earlier, after one of the guys had attempted to play a decade-old Urge Overkill record.

"Today," Chris said finally, nodding at the assembled cluster, "those guys figured out how to merge tables in a data set. And now…"

"Seriously," I agreed, even though I had no idea what he was talking about.

He finished his beer, set the bottle on the floor, and stood up. "Excuse me, darling," he announced, "but I'm going to head over there and see if I can be of any assistance." (Like lots of transplanted Southern ex-fraternity boys, Chris tended to start talking extra-fancy when he'd been drinking. It was deeply obvious, and I wished I didn't find it charming, but I did.)

"Okay, Buster," I said, to his back. I stayed on the couch for a couple more minutes and then wandered over to the other side of the apartment to smoke a cigarette. I heard the stereo start up again, sputtering the opening strains of "Positive Bleeding" as I went.

Because I don't *actually* smoke, I approached the best looking boy standing by the big bay windows and asked him if he had an extra; he said he didn't, but offered to share the one he'd just lit. His name, he announced, was Connor, which I thought sounded fake, so I told him that mine was Colleen. (It isn't.) After we'd smoked his cigarette all the way down to the filter, he nonchalantly pulled a nearly full pack of Parliaments from his pocket and lit us another. He was only twenty-two, it turned out, and so tall that he had to bend over to hear me every time I spoke; I left him and went to look for Chris when I got sick of repeating myself.

I found him in the kitchen, slicing limes next to a stack of shot glasses. "I thought you were sick of breaking *boys* in," he said, not looking up. It was true: I had said as much over late-night beers about a month before, after a dinner date during which a guy just two years my junior had ordered the rigatoni and then proceeded, before he'd consent to eat even a single bite, to pluck the peas from his pasta and line them up in a jiggling green semicircle around the edge of his bread plate. But I decided to pretend that I didn't have any idea what Chris meant or, better still, that I hadn't heard him at all.

"Salt?" I asked, instead.

"Behind you, on the second shelf."

I turned around to see a row of sideways-stacked cereal boxes, which I stared at for maybe twenty seconds before I finally spotted them: two small ceramic shakers, one black, one white, posed next to the Honey Nut Cheerios. They were shaped like little ghosts, their blobby arms extended, tucked together in a tender porcelain embrace. As I reached for the white one, I hesitated; I felt like an asshole for tearing them apart. Finally, I placed Casper on the counter, and Chris shot me a crooked grin, as though he'd somehow known exactly what I'd been thinking about.

"And the tequila," he said.

There was a makeshift bar set up in the corner—a folding card table cluttered with half-empty liquor bottles—but I was already drunk enough that none of the labels made any sense. I leaned low over them, looking closely, until a fat, pale hand grazed my shoulder, floated down in front of me, and grasped the Cuervo bottle just inches from my nose. Startled, I straightened suddenly and spun around, but the hand stayed where it was, so when I turned, I turned into its owner's arms. It was like we'd been dancing and I'd just closed a twirl, except, of course, that the guy was grasping a big bottle of tequila instead of the small of my back. I regained my balance and stepped away from him as quickly as I possibly could.

He introduced himself, incredibly, *as* Chris's boss. I couldn't believe it. I looked at Chris over The Boss's shoulder, and he rolled his eyes, but only a little bit. I got the message: I'd be nice.

But The Boss was a world of not-my-type. He had blond hair that stuck straight up off of his blotchy forehead and metal-framed glasses that kept sliding down his nose; the thick lenses magnified his watery blue eyes, making him look like an astigmatic cartoon bug. He was wearing a white button-down shirt with vertical dark and light-blue stripes, tucked—in the front only—into a pair of pleated khakis. The hand that wasn't holding the tequila was inexplicably clutching a small box of wooden toothpicks.

Chris stopped slicing and lined up the shots. We consumed them. He poured out another round, and we drank those too. Helplessly, I started giggling; straight liquor still tastes like high school to me. Chris poured the tequila again, and, just as I was getting ready to drink it, he reached across the counter, caught my left hand, and pulled it close to his face. Slowly, he licked the salt off the inside of my wrist. When his tongue touched my skin, it shot a shock through my body; it felt like a string had been stretched between the veins in my wrist and the deepest part of my stomach, and he'd tugged it. Then, still holding my hand, he tipped his tequila straight into his mouth, swallowed it, slammed the glass down, and grinned. Laughing, I slipped a lime between his lips.

The Boss just stood there, staring. After a few seconds, he started trying to talk to Chris about something boring—office politics, maybe—

and Chris turned away and let go of my hand. I took my last shot, and then decided it might be (or, at least, *look*) fun to dance. So I started out into the crowd alone, leaving the two of them in the kitchen by the butcher block. As I left, I grabbed another slice of lime and pressed it to my tongue. It tasted sweet and a little bit sour.

Someone had, rather sensibly, swapped out the overly earnest grunge music of our collective adolescence in favor of the party-friendly pop of our carefree early youth. I spun, slightly aimlessly, across the center of the dance floor until an old Prince song came on and The Boss appeared, asking if I'd ever heard of Morris Day. I wasn't anywhere near invested enough to answer him honestly, so I said no and spun again. But on my way back around, I realized that I'd miscalculated: he was the sort to take my apparent ignorance as an opportunity. He loomed beside me still, and as soon as I made even a second's worth of eye contact, he started in about The Time.

Everyone at those parties always thinks I'm Chris's girlfriend, but The Boss seemed to know that I was not—he instigated, and then dominated, a needlessly lengthy conversation that made no reference to Chris whatsoever. Instead, he talked about his record collection, and where he went to college, and—for some reason—his childhood dog, a terrier named Tuffy. I suppose he was trying to flirt with me, although I couldn't see it then. To be completely honest, I thought he was beneath me. The Internet boom may have conferred some kind of sudden cachet to his chosen career, but I wasn't taken in: I strongly suspected that The Boss had ended up in charge of an online gaming company only because he'd spent his high school years in the late 1980s locked in a basement somewhere, jacking off and posting to Dungeons and Dragons BBSes.

He never seemed, for a second, like someone I couldn't handle.

But when the cab pulled up to the curb opposite my apartment later that night, The Boss climbed out to let me by, and it took me a minute to right myself. By the time I did, I saw that he'd already shut the taxi door behind me and was passing a rolled-up twenty through the rolled-down front window, telling the driver to keep the change. Without waiting, I started off across the empty street, but The Boss followed. Inwardly, I shrugged. If he wanted to walk me to my door, I figured, fine.

◊

Three years back, not long after I moved to New York, I was almost attacked on my way into my apartment. I mean, I think I was. At least, that's what I tell people. I was walking back from a bar on 7th Street with my neighbors Dave and Rose, and, as we passed by the bodega on the corner of our block, I suddenly decided that I needed some milk, so I sent them on without me. I picked up a quart of two percent and a box of cookies—these fancy lattice-patterned butter wafers that my roommate Sebastian likes—and while I waited to pay, I petted the cashier's new kitten, which was sitting on the glass-topped counter next to the chewing gum and rolling papers, meowing softly at me. She was pure black and tiny, with one paw that looked like it had been dipped in something white, and her fur felt like smoke. As I left, I heard the cashier cooing at her, "It is you and I now, *gatita*, you and I," and for some reason I thought, *How romantic.*

Clearly, I was a little bit tipsy.

So when I got back to my building, instead of pulling the first of the heavy green-metal-and-glass doors closed behind me like I usually do, I simply stepped inside and let it swing lazily shut. Just as I was about to insert my keys into the second door's lock, I felt a big blast of warm air, like breath, from the street, and I turned around to find a tall, thin, empty-eyed man standing with me in the tiny, fluorescent-lit vestibule.

My pulse immediately sped to sprinting pace, but I tried hard not to look panicked. I had just finished reading this book by a bushy-mustached private investigator who was always on *Oprah* at the time; it was basically a manual of what to do in situations such as this. There were seventeen chapters, but they all boiled down to one simple thesis: Don't be afraid to act like a bitch. (Apparently, if you're mouthy enough, a lot of perverts will decide that you're just not worth the bother.) So I stood up as straight as I could and very loudly asked the guy what the hell exactly he was trying to do.

"It's cool, baby," he said. He slowly raised his right hand, palm open like he was being sworn in, apparently to demonstrate the lack of lethal weapons. "Don't be scared. I'm just here to see my friend."

"Who's your friend?" I demanded. My voice kept coming out shrill, even though I wanted it to sound calm and confident. His eyes flicked over to the short row of stainless steel mailboxes on the wall and then back to mine.

"John," he said.

I was absolutely certain that no one named John lived in my building, but for some reason it seemed like it would be worse to admit that. "Well, why don't you go back outside and buzz *John* then," I said, practically yelling. "Because following a girl into her building in the middle of the night? IS scary." I rested my right hand flat across the bank of buzzers, ready to hit every single button hard if he did anything other than turn around and leave.

"Alright, baby, alright," he said. Without lowering his palm, he pivoted and pushed the outside door open. I watched him start to wander off, then grabbed the handle and jerked it closed behind him. I ran up all four flights of stairs to my apartment, put the milk in the fridge, and got right into bed, still breathless, without washing my face or brushing my teeth. My heart was beating hard, and I couldn't seem to make it stop. It was summer, and through my open window I could hear someone below, in the building across the airshaft, fucking. I didn't hear a man, just a woman, moaning theatrically. It sounded, I decided, like she was faking.

But last night, when I unlocked the door and The Boss seized the handle, held it open for me, and then closed it with a soft click behind him, my pulse remained absolutely steady. He trailed me as I climbed the stairs, staying three or four steps below, maintaining a respectful distance. When I got to the top, he stopped on the second-to-last step and waited politely for me to stop jangling my keys. I held my breath as I inserted them into the lock, hoping to hear the microwave, the television, *anything* that would tell me that Sebastian was already home. But when I swung my apartment door open, everything inside was quiet and black.

It was The Boss who leaned through the doorway and flicked the light switch on the wall, electrifying the trio of bare bulbs that hung over the island in the kitchen. I stepped aside, allowing him to walk past me, and locked the bolt behind him—a reflex. We hadn't even spoken since the cab, since before Chris got out.

Now he was in my apartment, and I had no idea what to do with him. I didn't want him to be there. I didn't even understand what he thought he was *doing* there. In the past, the dynamics of my drunken hookups had been so finely calibrated that I can honestly say that this was the first time I'd ever been confronted, in my space, by someone who seemed to expect something from me that I didn't want to give. I wasn't certain what that meant I owed him.

So I offered him a drink.

"Sounds good," he said, heading towards the living room.

I pulled a short plastic tumbler from the drying rack by the sink and filled it nearly to the brim with Sebastian's scotch whiskey—no ice—and then took a long swig straight from the bottle before re-capping it; I didn't get myself a glass because I didn't want to seem overly companionable. I carried the cup to The Boss, accidentally sloshing a bit of liquor over the side as I handed it to him, and decided that after he'd drunk it, we would both be able to pretend like it was the only thing he came up there for, and he would leave with his dignity intact. But he didn't. Instead, he took two wincing sips and set the cup down on a coaster atop the coffee table, pushed his glasses up the bridge of his nose with his thumb, and moved in.

I'd situated myself as far from him as possible, on the corner of Sebastian's ancient couch, but rather than standing up as he came at me, I leaned back. I was still trying to duck his advance in a way that wouldn't make it too obvious that an advance had actually been made. Plausible deniability, I guess. It didn't work. The Boss, that bizarrely coordinated former computer-game champ, course corrected instantly, covering my mouth with his. His right hand landed flat on my collarbone, pinning me against the yellow velvet.

Only two weeks earlier, I'd sat cross-legged on that same mustard-colored cushion listening to a Built to Spill album—*There's Nothing*

Wrong With Love—with Chris's head in my lap. We'd gone to a Beastie Boys show with some guys we knew from school and, after the encore, Chris had asked if he could come home with me; something about his AC being broken. He said he wanted to stay over. He didn't say exactly where.

So, instead of sleeping, we sat on the couch and listened to music and talked about nothing, stifling our yawns, even though we were both tired and it was very late. I had the distinct feeling that it would be rude to go to bed without him, yet I wasn't about to be the one to issue an invitation. Eventually, he told me to scoot over, and laid his head across my thighs. I shifted, slightly uncomfortable at first, and placed my hand lightly on his crown. And as I sat there, running my fingers through his hair, I stared at the switched-off television set and tried to decide if we'd finally wandered out of the range of behavior that can be considered completely normal for two people who really are just friends.

When I looked down at him, his eyes were already on mine. He said, quietly, "So, what do you think, kid?"

I waited. "About what?"

He didn't answer.

The album ended, and the speakers went quiet, and still, Chris kept looking at me, but I didn't lower my lips to his. Yes, of course I wanted to kiss him. But, much more, I wanted him to kiss me first. When that didn't happen, I found that I couldn't keep up my end of our staring contest; I looked away, and the silence stretched out between us.

It was what they call a pregnant pause. I wanted to abort it.

◊

So, that's one thing I had to give The Boss: he wasn't lacking in initiative. He pointed his tongue, like a finger, and pressed it against my lips; I wondered, almost idly, whether he'd leave me alone if I unsealed them—if I let him in, just a little bit.

His right hand deserted my clavicle in favor of my left breast, which was bare under my cream-colored silk blouse (and easily accessed, it turned out, through my low-cut V-neck). His left hand alighted on my right leg and started to slither up under my denim miniskirt.

It occurred to me that despite his advanced age—he looked to be at least thirty—The Boss might not have that much experience; this, I figured, explained how he could miss my very clear signals of *un*-interest. And, yes, I still hadn't actually *said* anything to him. I think I was afraid that if I said no, and he ignored me, it would somehow render even less endurable what I feared was going to happen anyway. Plus, I wasn't a total idiot: When he pushed my underwear to the side, ripping it along a seam, and penetrated me roughly with his fingers, there was an unmistakable undercurrent of barely-controlled acquisitiveness.

Sometimes, when I've been drinking, I lose the last few minutes before I fall asleep. It's usually just a forgotten conversation with Sebastian about whatever boy he's currently obsessing over, or maybe the misplaced resolution of an after-midnight movie. Once, I woke up with a half-eaten honey-dipped donut perched, like a present, on the pillow next to me.

That night, the last thing I could remember was The Boss going into the bathroom—to wash his hands, I guess, after he'd finished with me. When I came to the next morning, I was alone. A quick, desperate scan of the empty left side of the bed—still neatly covered by my pulled-up comforter, and lacking the usual telltale indentations—seemed to suggest that I'd slept alone, too. But I couldn't really be certain of that. Gingerly, I raised my white duvet and peered underneath: I was naked, save for the theoretically skin-colored band-aids that crisscrossed my bloodless breasts, a utilitarian (if half-hearted) attempt at modesty that suddenly seemed far tawdrier to me than total nudity ever could.

I lay flat on my back with my hand on my stomach, which felt somehow hollow: simultaneously sucked in and scraped out. After a while, I moved my palm to my clavicle and curved my thumb and index finger around my neck, exactly as The Boss had done. I imagined my smallish hand fitting into a kind of shadow left by his larger one; it took only a tiny bit of added pressure, I discovered, to make me begin to feel as though my windpipe was being pushed shut.

The clothes I'd been wearing the previous evening were scattered, like breadcrumbs, across the bedroom floor; I located my cellphone under a skirt just as it was about to stop ringing. It was Chris. I'd barely begun to consider what I might tell him—the idea of saying nothing whatsoever was equal parts appealing and utterly impossible—but I pressed the button and lifted the phone to my ear without hesitation. We weren't in the habit of engaging in morning-after postmortems; if he was calling me this early, he already knew.

"Hey," he said.

"Hi. Hang on." I set the phone down on the pile of books that doubled as my nightstand and searched the floor for my underwear. It was missing. I pondered that for exactly as long as it took to retrieve a new pair from the top drawer of my dresser, and then I pulled them on, plus a T-shirt, and picked up the phone. "Hi," I said again.

There was a long pause.

"Are you okay?" he asked me.

"He called you?"

"Yeah."

"Gross." Suddenly, it occurred to me that Chris might actually know more about what had happened to me the night before than I did. I was almost certain that The Boss hadn't been anywhere near as drunk as I was—simply because it didn't seem scientifically possible—so it really just depended on the level of detail he might have enjoyed disseminating. "What did he tell you?"

"Honestly," he admitted, sidestepping my question, "I had a bad feeling as soon as I got out of that cab."

"You did?" I was perplexed because I hadn't felt anything. (It didn't occur to me until much later that Chris knew his employer far, far better than I did.) "Why?"

"You just looked so small," he said. "And then, when I talked to him this morning, he told me that *that* was when he realized you were interested. When I got out, and you stayed close."

I dropped the phone onto the bed and jogged towards the bathroom, suddenly beset by a sweaty billow of nausea; there, I retched unproductively over the toilet and then splashed cool water on my face, which looked, in the mirror, almost unreasonably well-rested. By the time I made it back to my bedroom, the cellphone was ringing again.

"Hello."

"I lost you," Chris said.

"I'm sorry."

"It's not *your* fault."

But it was, at least a little bit. I'd been as unrelentingly passive with The Boss as I'd always been with Chris and now—again, in spite of myself—I was waiting to see what he might say or do about it. "I should have just gotten out of the car and gone inside with you," I confessed. "That was what I wanted to do."

"Yeah...That was what I wanted too."

For what felt like a full minute, I listened to his breathing: It was so pronounced and so intimate that I could practically see him lying in his bed, his unclothed chest rising and falling under a threadbare top sheet. Unwillingly, I pictured my left shoulder fitting perfectly into the space between his extended right arm and his torso, my lips sighing against his throat.

"Look," he said. "I'm going to come over now. Is that okay? I'm going to buy you some pierogies. I'm going to take you out."

"Okay."

"If you want," he added, "you can even prank-call him. I have his number."

"No," I said immediately. "I don't want to do that." I wondered: Could he possibly think that *that* would constitute a proportionate response? I knew, of course, that I wasn't exactly going to be hightailing it down to the precinct to file a police report. But a part of me had begun to think, or maybe hope, that Chris might do *something* to defend my honor. If he knew what had happened, and he wasn't mad at me, how could he be anything less than furious at his boss? "What are you going to say to him," I asked, "when you get to work tomorrow?"

He was quiet for a moment—this time, I couldn't even hear him exhale. "He's engaged," he said finally. "I probably won't mention it."

◊

After we hung up, I washed my face again—with soap, this time—and started to apply blush, only to switch gears and climb into the shower, where I stood under the cold water for as long as I could tolerate it. (Not very long, as it happens—I'm not much of a stoic if there's no one there to see it.) Then I got dressed, combed my still-dripping hair, and used a licked Q-tip to remove the dark makeup that had collected under my lower lashes. I was already halfway down the stairs when I heard the buzzer erupting in my empty apartment.

Chris was leaning against a sickly looking municipal tree, his arms folded in front of his chest. He dropped them when he saw me, but I didn't approach him. Instead, I stopped in front of the door, a few yards away. Something about the situation reminded me of a standoff; in fact, I realized, we'd treated our whole relationship like a stickup, thinking that if nobody moved, nobody would get hurt. But it wasn't true. Obviously.

The pockmarked asphalt at Chris's feet still bore a stain caused by the deceased pigeon I'd found there a few weeks before (somehow, I'd never realized that birds contain red, aqueous blood exactly like a person's—usually, when you see one dead in the street, it's long since been flattened). Above his head, the tree's sparsely leaved branches were almost supernaturally still; the morning air felt stagnant, moist, and heavy, and I could tell that by noon it would be positively oppressive, ninety-five degrees and ninety-five percent humidity. Chris opened his mouth to speak and I turned away, preemptively. It was only mid-June, and the best part of the summer was already over.

Ramshackle Chandelier

Doug Paul Case

Baby, this is our golden age
and we'll have fire in, around

the light—burning against glass
so hot we'll melt back to sand,

slip with the hours, the sheets
crumpling from bedframes.

Like moths hatching,
we'll cling another moment

to the ropes, composing,
before something inside them,

or inside us, snaps—

Eternal Puckering

Tom Oristaglio

the eternal puckering
that seems to emanate
from the center of certain
homeless men, ad hoc
sonar of cork forced by knife butt
into wine bottle,
the kind kind of coughing,
the static of lettuce
always heaped to mask
the meager sandwich,
weak fixings, flabby anchors,
meandering entrails endearing
themselves to the clouds
with the battle-hardened gusto
of honorable men,
whose jelly ablaze!
whose napalm horses!
stretch this tether of absence
to the breaking point—
absence the only thing
that keeps us grounded—
so they breach its limits
and float away,

while our shadows glare up,
our effete, minigolf-playing
shadows:

shadows of swords to fall upon.

A Foursome Bowling

Peter Stenson

First Frame

Sandy Casoli loved the Bravo Network and Sudoku and was only so-so into bowling, but that's where she was, Split This!, a twenty-lane alley, a semi-forgotten relic to hair bands and wide-collared button-downs. She stood next to the ball dispenser. She held a ball, pink, but ugly pink, too soft, too washed out. Her husband, Daniel, told her to line it up with the arrows. She didn't acknowledge this with anything but the bobbing of her black ponytail. *Line it up with the arrows*, she mocked inside her head. Dick. She listened to his voice, the way it became deeper around other people, and he was giving encouragement and bits of advice and then it was comments about her taking all night and this, of course, was followed by a rip-roaring laugh, fake, a show, look-at-me-I'm-Funny-Husband, and sometimes, Sandy knew his worry and peptalks and smothering glances were because he loved her, but tonight wasn't one of those times.

She walked over to the lane. She didn't look at the arrows. She looked at the pins. She heaved the ball. It was heavier than she remembered. It started down the middle and veered a little to the left and with a soft thud, all but one pin fell.

Clapping from behind her and Sandy turned and Daniel was giving her a thumbs-up and Becca smiled her born-blonde smile and Jorge nodded. She said, See, girl's got game, and Daniel was like, It was great baby, now just aim a little…

Sandy's ball burped out of the retriever and she picked it up. She inserted her fingers. She thought about getting the last pin down and the big to-do Daniel would make out of a strike or spare or whatever the hell it was called, and then she thought about the reason Daniel had been pushing this double so hard—her sobriety, wanting some of Becca to rub off on her, the cork in the jug, twelve steps, for Sandy to experience some of the *joy of living* as Daniel had started calling it over the last eighteen months of his non-drinking—and Sandy didn't aim, just walked and heaved, only kind of caring if her tired pink struck anything.

It did.

The pin fell.

◊

Jorge Rodriguez looked more black than Hispanic and had been dubbed Thunder Stick his one semester as an Alpha Phi Alpha at U-Michigan and never threw without his Storm Gadget XF Wrist Support (southpaw)—a gunmetal plastic sheathing that stretched from the girth of his forearm to the tip of his index. A wicked case of tendinitis in his late twenties (orthopedically scoped) had led him to find wrist support, and now, at thirty-five, he couldn't roll without it. He never questioned if this was a physical or mental restraint.

As he rose from the orange plastic chair, his wife, Becca, pulled at the hem of his black tee. She mouthed *remember*. He nodded. He wasn't retarded. They'd just spent the fifteen-minute drive discussing his expected etiquette—to be *a part of*, to understand that they were couples *having fun bowling*, not merely *bowling*—and he'd assured her that it was all good. He'd abide by her rules. But she'd kept going. Kept talking about his competitive streak. He'd gotten quiet then. The highway had been specks of red lights. She'd said that she knew he'd be great. She'd taken his hand, bringing it to her mouth, kissing his knuckles. He'd glanced at his knuckles. They'd been covered in a bright shade of early middle age.

Jorge rolled a Brunswick Wicked Siege. He loved it. The ball was an optical illusion in color—either purple or black depending upon overhead lighting—with a tasteful silver etching of Dr. Doom's metal facemask. He felt like it made a statement. Something aggressive. Something powerful. Something that merged the ball and him as one.

He lined his left foot four inches behind the dot on the thirty-board. He brought the ball to its birthplace, exactly three inches out from his clavicle and four inches from his left earlobe. This was the moment he loved. The quiet and stillness of this five seconds. When it was just you and the ball and the pins. The feel of Doom was just the right amount of heavy. The pinch of his fingers was just the right amount of pain. He felt the world drop away. His vision narrowed, tunneled. It settled on the thirty-board arrow. Every nerve ending in his body remembered the feeling of a perfect throw.

He was milliseconds away from starting his right foot forward—from starting the motion that had once been described as *breathtaking in its fluidity*—when he heard the voice of his wife telling Sandy and Daniel how *silly Jorge's bowling obsession was.*

His weight was already in motion. He couldn't stop thinking about this being a bitchy thing to say. Why would she say this during my approach? Does she have no respect for me? For bowling? Jorge thought about her warnings in the car. How she thought bowling was merely a social activity. Something he did twice a week with his friends to blow off steam. Jorge told himself to stop because his mind wasn't clear. He didn't. He kept going. He thought about Becca not even trying to understand what it all meant to him. Not caring in the slightest. He let the ball go. The turnover of his wrist felt good. The wax job was perfect and grabbed the ball, and it increased velocity with each rotation until it hooked directly into the pocket. The pins exploded into the backdrop.

Damn, that's good, he thought.

Jorge knew it was a rare night. He told himself not to think about it—the unobtainable three hundred—but he did. His stroke just felt that good.

Daniel Casoli sold bulk airfare to third-rate destinations like Gulfport and Laughlin and had performed cunnilingus on Becca six hours earlier in Room 107 at the Lake Ilene Inn after the noon AA meeting and he'd told her it was love, what they were doing, how he felt, and she'd said something along the same lines, and that's when he'd suggested bowling, *let's do it, a double, just to be with you.*

So here he was, his arm around his wife, his eyes darting between Jorge, smug in his obvious skill on the lanes, and Becca, the blonde Ritz Carlton of his life. His wife took a slug of beer, finishing the plastic cup before the first frame. The smell of beer still gave him somewhat of a moist tongue. He'd asked her to maybe take it easy with the drinking tonight. This was in the parking lot on their way in, their arms intertwined. She'd said, Yeah, keep that in mind.

See I have some work to do, he said to the group.

Jorge smiled. He had giant lower teeth, freakish really, bigger than Daniel had ever seen. Jorge said, Just luck, brother, just luck.

Go, Sandy said.

I'm going, I'm going.

Daniel stood and tried to make his last glance meaningful and have it be with Becca and it was, both with her and meaningful, and Daniel felt like the looks they shared—first across the decaying Uptown Alano Club from over the rims of white Styrofoam coffee cups, months later across forkfuls of strawberry and brie salad at the Lexington, her telling him about the *miracle of the mundane* and *letting go and letting God* and the *joy of living clean and sober*, and then just two months ago, the look they shared in Room 107 for the first time, the guilt of breaking vows and taboos and the excitement and the secure knowledge that what they were doing was okay because their partners didn't understand what it was like to battle a foe more cunning and baffling than cancer—were better than anything, a secret, an understanding.

Aim at the pins, Sandy said.

The arrows, honey.

For reals, yo.

Daniel Casoli took his ball, an ungodly heavy black house ball, and brought it to his chin. Becca called out something about seeing those skills. This made him smile, his back to his wife, his grin visible to nobody except the ball, and he aimed at the center arrow. He thought about the way Becca had crushed her nearly perfect thighs around his head that afternoon, how this had created a seashore sound, waves crashing, waves receding.

He tossed his ball.

It knocked eight pins down, the two on the far right still standing.

He turned. Sandy poured another beer from the pitcher. She said, Arrows, babe, arrows.

He gave her a placating smile. She gave him a mocking thumbs-up.

He picked up his ball from the dispenser and sometimes he wondered if he still loved Sandy and he held the ball inches from his mouth and thought about her being so selfish to continue to drink the way she did after everything that had happened, after how hard he'd worked at quitting, and there she was, pounding Budweisers like it was the Armageddon, in front of Becca, nonetheless, even after the talk about her taking it easy tonight. He started his approach. Daniel wondered how to broach the subject with Becca. He didn't want to be the one who suggested they leave their partners. The ball hit the two pins. Daniel pumped his fist.

◊

Becca Joyce-Rodriquez was the youngest of four sisters and couldn't fully bring herself to sing in the shower, settling for a continuous hum, telling herself it was just as good, and to her, bowling was Jorge's thing, always had been, always would be, and she was beginning to think this whole evening was a gross miscalculation on her part. Daniel's wife was getting salty, Jorge hadn't said but two words, and Daniel, bless his heart, wouldn't stop staring.

Bowling with some regular old pros, she said.

Maybe Jorge here, Daniel said. He slapped Jorge on the shoulder. Becca knew this was a mistake, that Jorge hated being touched. She went to squeeze her husband's hand but was greeted by his bionic arm. Then it was Sandy draining another glass and peering at Becca, saying things about wrist guards and arrows, and Daniel had been right, her drinking *was* bad. They'd been there…what, twenty minutes, and she was already openly mocking her husband.

No wonder he cheats.

Seriously, she said, you guys are some rock star bowlers.

Then you're in good company, Daniel said. He seemed to be trying to keep his stare and she wished he would stop with that. Jorge wasn't stupid. Neither was Sandy. Daniel just staring, staring, always, and she'd wanted to say *what*? What is so interesting? What are you trying to say? Use your words. Just stop looking.

Go baby, Jorge said.

Becca got up. She felt everyone's eyes on her—her husband's and Daniel's and Sandy's, but also the gazes of the group of teenagers the next lane over, the fifty-something's two lanes from them—and that's how it'd always been. Becca the object of affection. Becca the baby of the family, her father's cheekbones, her mother's curves. She thought about her first dates with Jorge, him standing behind her, teaching her how to roll, how his warm breath was both repulsive and endearing. She lifted up her ball. It was lavender, a present from Jorge when he still tried to get her to bowl. She wanted to keep up with a strike. She heard Daniel bark bits of encouragement. She thought about how he'd finally said I love you earlier that afternoon and she'd had no idea how to react. She'd looked down between her legs. It was just Daniel's eyes peeking over the bald mound of her pelvis. She'd wanted to go back five minutes, to redirect the afternoon and their actions and then maybe two months before that and refuse to grab lunch and then months and months back, her choosing a different home group, her not confusing attention for esteem, and then she wanted to keep going back and to learn to control her drinking before it became daily and then she'd be a kid, her father's baby, putting her ear between the snaps of his flannel shirt, forgetting about sight, just listening to his breaths, his laughs, his little hairs tickling the cavern of her ear.

She bowled.

It made a beeline for the gutter.

Shit.

That's okay, Daniel said.

Use the arrows, yo, Sandy said.

Jorge grinned, gave a wink.

Her next shot hit the middle of the pins. Seven of them toppled over, the eighth undecided, teetering, settling on staying put.

Fifth Frame

Here's to the shitty-ass game of bowling, Sandy said.

She raised her plastic cup, a Budweiser Lime logo on its side, her fifth. Nobody raised their glasses and she said, Figures, yo, and she smiled at Jorge because he understood being confined in the prison of holier-than-thou marital sobriety. She said, Now we're onto some shit, huh, and Daniel placed his hand on her back, but it was more controlling than loving.

So I'm just going to go ahead and throw it out there, she said. Bro, what's up with the wrist thing?

Jorge cited something about an injury.

Because I'm like Transformer Arm is straight up killing it, you know? Maybe need one of those things myself.

You're up, honey.

No shit.

Well?

The pressure of his backrub increased.

Silly me. Thought we were here to socialize. I mean, that's what it's about, right, bowling? Talking. Am I wrong?

Absolutely, Becca said. That's what I've been telling Jorge here.

Sandy watched her lean over and kiss her husband's check, and she wondered how her own skin would look against his, the contrast, if she'd look paler or darker.

My girl knows what's up, Sandy said. She raised her glass and then laughed, saying, My bad.

Are you going to go, Daniel asked.

Are you going to dig your fingernail through my spine?

Sandy watched her husband play that one off like it was a joke, the two of them in on it, the two of them such tricksters, always giving one another hard times. He let out a nice laugh, loud and fake. But she could tell she'd pushed him far enough because the edges of his nostril were flaring and that's what happened when he became flustered and then she felt bad, seeing her husband on the loving side of the spectrum, almost like another human being.

She finished the flat backwash in her cup. She reached for the pitcher. It was empty. She said, Damn Jorge, slow your roll.

Was all you, hon, Becca said.

This pissed Sandy off because it was really her saying you're a fucking drunk slut and Sandy told herself it wasn't worth it, saying something back, stooping to their level—I'm-a-better-person-than-you-because-I'm-sober—so she said the next thing that crossed her mind: Shit ain't going to fill itself.

Becca looked down into her lap. Daniel's hand slid off her back. Jorge just sat there boring as fuck. And then she felt stupid because she'd done something wrong, that much was obvious. She just didn't know what. And this was happening more and more and she stood then, laughing, saying, Jesus, not like I fiddled a little boy, and grabbed the pitcher and headed towards the bar.

◊

Jorge lied to his wife, telling her he'd had two glasses, although he really was still on his first. She kept saying are you sure, are you sure? He nodded. He didn't want to talk. He didn't want to wait for drunk Sandy to come back and continue her attempts at ruining his perfect game—*don't put the* p *label on it*—but he knew that a confrontation between anyone would be detrimental to what he had going.

Baby, I could have sworn you only had one glass.

Jorge glanced at Daniel who quickly averted his gaze. Jorge felt bad for him. His wife was acting like an idiot. And now, he had to sit there pretending like he wasn't hearing Becca slander his wife.

Jorge, please, go ahead and bowl. It's no big deal, Daniel said.

Not a problem.

Serious. Who knows how long she'll be.

Jorge thought about this offer. Maybe the rest of them would drop out too. He'd be able to concentrate, really focus. He was five frames in, five perf—, five *solid* frames into a game, and it was closer than he'd ever been. But he also knew that any variance in the routine could cause the whole thing to implode.

I'm sorry, she's not normally like this, Daniel said.

Do you want me to talk to her, Becca asked.

No. I don't know. No, not tonight.

She's fine, Jorge said.

Maybe I should go…you know. Daniel stood. Becca nodded. Jorge just wanted them to figure it out, to get back down there, to continue with the game.

Once Daniel was out of earshot, Becca turned to Jorge. Her face was a pinched *what the fuck*. She said, Can you be anymore of a jerk?

What?

We talked about this. I mean, god, you've said all of ten words.

You're kidding me?

I wish.

Jorge shook his head. He couldn't believe he somehow had ended up as the bad guy. He told himself that he couldn't be distracted and that's what this fight would be. He envisioned his roll. The flawless gliding of foot and knee and arm and wrist, just the right amount of rollover, the pins exploding.

You always do this, Becca said.

Jorge wouldn't take the bait. He adjusted the gauge on his wrist protector.

Just tune out. Pretend you aren't even here. I mean, for once, that's all I asked, just this once to be sociable.

Jorge couldn't take the chance of responding because coiled on the tip of his tongue were insults he'd shelved for years. How could she be so clueless? So selfish to not understand the stakes of what he had going? It'd been the one thing he'd strived for his entire life. He looked at the score screen. Strike after strike after strike. He got up and started walking away.

Becca said, That's nice. Walk away. That's good.

Jorge climbed the three carpeted steps. He looked behind the register and a guy he only knew by mustache shook his head as if to say I see what you have going here. And beyond the register, he could make out Sandy at the bar, Daniel at her side, his hands pleading. He thought about all the games he'd rolled in his life—thousands, each one in the pursuit of a single goal—and he thought about his two-fifty-nine being his high. He thought about Becca making this sliver of a chance about her. *You're not doing this, you're not doing that.* He showed up when and where he was asked. He loved her with a care and tenderness that weren't natural for him, but as soon as they'd been alone, she'd started in with Sandy, with him, with everyone but herself. And walking into the men's room, he let himself think for the first time that life was better when his wife was still a drunk because at least he could give her selfishness an excuse.

◊

The bathroom door swung into the wall when Daniel Casoli walked in. He saw Jorge pissing at the far end of the trough and this made him annoyed, wanting a brief moment to regroup, splash some water on his face, pop an Altoid.

Some game you've got going out there, he said.

Oh. Thanks.

Daniel walked to the far side of the four-foot basin. He took out his penis. He said, I mean, you could be looking at a perf—

Ahh!

This sudden yell halted Daniel's stream. What the hell? Then he realized it was probably like baseball, how nobody mentioned a potential no-hitter while it was in progress.

Sorry, Daniel said.

It's fine.

They pissed. Clumps of chew littered the metal trough. Daniel couldn't help get the feeling that Jorge's piss was coming towards him, and it was, the angle designed that way, but its gushing felt somehow violent.

About everything, Daniel said. I don't know what's going on with Sandy. She normally isn't like this...and, I don't know...sorry I guess.

Daniel wished his mouth would just stop moving. That he would quit with the blanket apologies. He wondered if he really was apologizing for *it*—the fact he'd just been with Jorge's wife that very afternoon, that it had been going on for two months, that declarations of love had been exchanged, that it was only a matter of time until he would take Becca as his lover, rightfully so, legally, in front of the eyes of God, forever. But guilt wasn't part of it, not when what he and Becca had was so *right.* Sure, feelings would be hurt, both Jorge's and Sandy's, but it was different, what they had, their love like that of movies.

The piss streaming down the trough was a late-season harvest gold. Daniel didn't really realize he was doing it, following the liquid to its riverhead, but he was, and there *it* was, the biggest penis he'd ever seen in person. Holy shit. And just as involuntarily, he was then glancing at his own modest German-sized member, and his mind was the drain in the trough and it was jealousy at the vision of Becca loving that *thing* over there and it housing itself inside of where he'd been in Room 107 and then it was the thoughts of him never really satisfying Becca, that he'd understood this at a base level, that's why he'd spent so much time downstairs with his mouth, and he pictured husband and wife doing husband and wife things, and he could practically feel the thundering post-urination shakes of Jorge as he finished up an arms-length away and he *was* perfect—his perfect penis and perfect game—and Daniel told himself that it was different because he shared the same feelings as Becca, the need to numb oneself in the whirlpool of drink, to escape, to be somebody else, to feel appreciated for hour-long lunch dates, to simply connect. Jorge said he'd see him back out there. Daniel finished the last bit of his delicate stream. He knew that he had to be the one to put his cards on the table—Becca, I want to be with you, for real—and it had to be tonight.

Becca sat there on the rigid orange chair. The alley had filled up, every lane taken. People cheered and hollered and she studied the teenagers to her left with their sagged skinny jeans and sweeping bangs. She remembered that time. How things were all in the future tense. And then Becca looked at the fifties on the other side. They were more subdued, rhythmic in their head nods and high-fives, but they seemed happy in routine, in each other. And then Becca thought about being thirty-three, how it wasn't young and it wasn't old, and it was a phony age, one when they were supposed to have their shit together career-wise, family-wise, kids, budding 401Ks, weeklong trips over the summer to Colorado, camping, cheap and fun, and the sun rising over fourteen-thousand-foot peaks, their own memories. Nobody seemed to be looking at her. And then she thought about a saying in AA—*feeling alone in a crowd of a thousand*—and she'd fought with this mindset her entire life, and it was more AA clichés—*to be uniquely alone, trudging the road to happy destiny*—and she wondered if everyone felt these things, not just those who'd fucked up their lives with alcohol. And maybe bowling was invented so people could escape from this crushing weight for ten dollars and a few hours. Leagues and routine and being a regular or an activity or double date or an outing, all of it a distraction as good as an affair or glass of red.

Leave for five minutes and my girl looks like she's 'bout to slit her wrists, Sandy said. She stood at the end of the four-person table, fresh pitcher in hand.

Becca felt something close to relief at another person.

Where the boys?

Restroom.

Playing swords, huh?

Sorry?

Sandy laughed. She sat down and poured herself what had to be her sixth drink. Becca watched how her eyes closed when the cup touched her lips. She imagined the tickle of the bubbles jumping from the cup. She knew what Sandy felt. She did. That it was the only way, a reward for working, for living, for socializing, for making it this long on the earth.

There's a different way, Becca said.

What's up?

A different way, then...She pointed at the cup.

Sandy smirked. She trained her eyes directly into Becca's. She said, Knew this was coming.

I'm not here to lecture or—

No, no. Go ahead. Let's hear it. Really. I mean, that's why we're sitting here, right? The whole bowling thing. The boys *disappearing*. For this moment, the one where you tell me about twelve steps and powerlessness. How great life is. How'm I doing so far?

Think you have it all figured out?

Sandy shook her head. She said, Nope, not at all. But I'm not sitting here fronting like I do.

Becca fought the urge to tell her that she'd made her husband come that very day, that he'd professed his love for her, not Sandy, that maybe this was due to Sandy's drinking, her disregard for what Daniel was going through. Instead, she said, Funny, because that's what you seem to be doing. Telling me what I'm going to do, just like you have it all figured out.

Sandy leaned back, stretching, pushing her breasts out, and then rested both elbows on the table dividing them. She said, Listen, you seem like a nice enough woman. Really, you do. But I'll be motherfucked if I let you sit there passing judgments about being better than me.

That's not what I'm saying.

Then what is it?

That you don't need to drink like you do. That's it. That's all I have to say.

So I can be like…you? That it? Stop drinking, pray to God, go on pretending life is some magical fucking quest?

Never mind.

Or is it so I can have your life? That's what you all say, huh? *Want what she has?* So you want me to see you with your trashy push-up bra with the lace showing, your hundred-dollar haircut, your *ethnic* husband who doesn't talk, and frankly, seems to like bowling a whole lot more than you, and all of this is supposed to make me see the errors of my ways, make me jealous?

Nobody had ever talked to Becca like this before. She had no idea how to respond. She caught herself dabbing at the corner of her right eye and she told herself she would not be reduced to tears. Sandy wasn't worth it. She wasn't worth anything. Certainly not Daniel's affection or faithfulness. Becca felt like everyone in the entire alley was staring, was waiting for her to finally let go, to snap, to become something other than what she was, and she spoke from unmoving lips: I feel sorry for you.

Sandy reached across the table. She patted Becca's hand. She said, No, honey, least I know I'm a mess. You, babe, haven't the slightest fucking idea.

◊

Tenth Frame

Sandy looked at the overhead scoreboard and was like thank fucking god this night is almost over. She laughed at her scores, each turn basically a little worse than the previous. She didn't really care that her ball was a shitty shade of pink.

She lined up like she'd seen Jorge do, his feet just behind the dots. She realized Daniel had quit with the advice and encouragement, and this made her pause. She lost a step of balance and regained it, the ball almost dropping, her almost dropping, and she turned around and said, Walking's new to this bitch, and she was met by three smiles, each one the same, each one lifeless, pencil drawings on plastic mannequins. This was the image she started forward with. People becoming distant. People not really people. People just there to humor her, to tell her good job, maybe next time, you have such potential, that's okay.

Her ball traveled the length of the lane in the gutter.

She turned and Daniel didn't say anything, barely made eyes, and Jorge studied his stupid wrist thing, and that bitch Becca stared off at the middle-aged grouping to their right. Sandy walked off the actual lanes. She wedged her way between her husband's knees. She said, Any pointers, Daddy?

He shook his head.

Come on, what am I doing wrong?

Again it was the shaking of his head and this felt like a betrayal because that's who Daniel was, the supportive husband, the caretaker, the advice giver, and he wouldn't engage, wouldn't even tell her about the arrows, so that's what she said, running the back of her fingernails down his check, What was that thing about the arrows?

He turned his face away from her touch. He said, Please just finish.

Sandy gave a snort. She said, Fun night. She took her ball and she held it and she wanted her husband to tell her what she needed to do to succeed. For him to say something that indicated he still gave a fuck. She studied the largest arrow in the middle of the lane. She'd bowl it straight. She'd bowl it down the middle and knock the pins over. And then it was the thoughts that she'd pushed him too far, like all he asked was for her to keep it under control, that this night meant a lot to him, and she aimed with every morsel of concentration and took three steps and let the ball go.

It started straight. It ended up in the gutter.

And Sandy thought this was the best she could do and maybe it wasn't good enough and she didn't want to face Daniel because he'd moved on from trying and his mouth would be that tight-lipped smile or even worse, nothing at all, so she stayed facing the lanes and felt the reverberation of bowled balls from the wood through her shoes and then she felt the music too.

Jorge's first roll of the tenth frame was perfect—*go ahead and say it, perfect*—the pins not having a chance at staying upright. He was two rolls away from The Unobtainable. Two rolls away from dropping the *un*, from becoming one of nine other people he knew of in the Twin Cities to reach the fabled three hundred. To reach perfection.

Come on, baby, you can do it, Becca said.

He wouldn't turn around. Didn't want to mess with his concentration.

She'd changed her tune, her angry-wife-you-need-to-be-different comments because she'd probably finally understood what was happening, what he was about to accomplish. A lifetime achievement. He loved her for understanding or at least pretending to.

Four inches behind the dot on the thirty-board.

Envision the approach, the release, the follow-through, everything smooth, molasses sliding down a glass jar.

Doom settled into the lane with a love-tap spanking and hugged the gutter and then curved and kept curving and it was going to be perfect, just south of the backside of the One. The pins tumbled.

People cheered. The lanes to either side had quit and now just watched. The workers stood behind him. People raised their fists. A few clapped. A catcall sounded from a few lanes over. Becca held her hands in front of her face as if praying. And it was Jorge talking to himself, trying to block out the building tension, the buzz of hushed voices, of excitement at witnessing the amazing—*concentrate, this is you, you can do this, one more roll.* He picked up his ball. He rubbed down the metal mask etched into its purple-black surface. He spoke to it, the ball, his persona, the silent title he'd dubbed himself, Doom. We can do this. Just give me this. God, please, just give me this. He wondered if they weren't one in the same, God and his ball, a silent object there to be manipulated to do as he wanted.

He lined up.

Please, Doom, this is our time.

He ratcheted one more degree of support from his Storm Gadget XF Wrist Support.

And then it was quiet. The gathered crowd ceased to exist. His wife's calls and Daniel's stares and Sandy's drunken slurs were all gone—his life boiled down to him versus ten plastic pins. Doom radiated pure fucking love and destruction and empathy. He prayed for them all and channeled every game played and every ball rolled and every pin struck. He started forward. His release felt perfect. Life in slow motion. Everything crumbled away to him alone with Doom. The two of them could conquer anything. The two of them were lovers and friends, and that's all he needed and ever would, and this was what everything he'd ever worked for amounted to. He watched his best friend travel the sixty feet. Then it happened—the pins fell, each and everyone of them.

Jorge dropped to his knees. His eyes filled. He heard screaming and cheering, and it was just noise. He dreaded the back slaps and hugs he knew were coming. He never wanted to move. To be anywhere else. For it all to end. He watched the mechanical arm come down, clear his pins into the backdrop. He wondered if this was as good as it got. Ten fresh pins were put in their place. It was over that fast, everything he'd ever wanted, perfection.

◊

Their game was interrupted with strangers congratulating Jorge. Daniel watched as the owner came out, a hairy man, not altogether unlike a pin himself, and shook Jorge's hand, presenting him with a small plaque with *300* engraved on its golden surface.

Becca sat back down after kissing her husband. Daniel thought about Jorge's giant penis between those lips, the same set he'd kissed earlier. And it was too much, this thought, Becca with anyone else, sexually or physically or emotionally, and she'd said it that day—I love you, too.

All that was left of Sandy was a plastic cup. She'd gone off to return her shoes. Daniel thought that her missing out on everything was fitting. Just like it'd been over the last eighteen months with her drinking, her not growing, not changing, and Daniel experiencing life for the first time without the inebriation of alcohol, without being numb, and that was it, he thought, simple as that—I've grown into a different person.

He made eyes at Becca. She smiled, her lipstick still evenly applied. And it was now or never because they couldn't go on living this lie and double life. But that was bullshit, because it wasn't about guilt, but about sharing his new life with a woman who understood.

He leaned across the table. Becca glanced over at Jorge, still being congratulated. Daniel said, We need to talk.

What?

Talk. Us. About us.

Not now, Becca said. She glanced back at her husband.

I can't do this anymore, the lying. I need to…to be—

Stop, okay?

I need to be with you.

Becca laughed. It was beautiful and hurtful and he had no idea what was funny and he took her hand and she tried to pull away but he held her firm, his fingers cinched around her tiny wrist.

We can't keep doing this. It's not fair, to them. We need to let—

Becca yanked her hand free. She said, You need to stop.

Becca's coldness wasn't making sense and he tried to meet her gaze, to communicate through silent understanding. Her attention darted between Jorge and Daniel and her cuticles. Baby, Daniel said. She shook her head. He thought about her doing the same thing against the pillow earlier that afternoon and he said, You, I choose you, and her head kept shaking, and this wasn't supposed to be happening because he'd worked so hard in his new life and it was all for her, he understood that, the DUI, the meetings, Sandy's drinking, all of it to get him into that Tuesday noon meeting months before, to get him to the woman who returned his stare, who spoke of love without having to open her mouth.

I'm not going to leave, she said.

What?

Jorge. I won't.

Becca, what we have—

Is nothing. A fantasy. An excuse.

With that, she stood, walking over to Jorge, throwing her arms around him, standing on her tiptoes, kissing his chin. Daniel kept thinking this isn't right, not even a little bit, and he replayed the conversation, his words, hers, and she'd said love, she'd fucking said it not seven hours before, and he felt a hand on his shoulder and for the briefest of moments he let himself believe it was Becca's, her French-manicured fingers rubbing his back, telling him it was okay, they'd figure it out, that she was sorry she'd hurt his feelings.

The fuck's going on, Sandy said.

Daniel shrugged. He leaned his head into his wife's stomach. She petted his hair.

There Becca stood under her husband's arm, the entire alley still watching, still coming up for a fist bump or handshake. And she smiled. She smiled and smiled and smiled because maybe life and marriage were this easy, to stand by the side of her partner soaking in the leftover stares. She glanced at Daniel. Sandy rubbed his hair. He'd get over it. And she thought about what it'd meant and maybe it was as simple as wanting to know she still had it or maybe it was that Jorge didn't pay her enough attention or maybe it was because Daniel had made her feel special. That's it. Special. That's all she'd ever fucking wanted. To matter. And she rested her head in the nook of her husband's chest and it was her father in those quiet childhood moments and she looked at their resting balls—black and purple-black and off-pink and lavender—and they sat in a straight line, their slicked sides touching.

She spoke into Joge's black T-shirt: You love me?

He didn't say anything. He stared at the electronic monitor hanging from the ceiling. Red block letters flashed *!PERFECT!* He probably didn't hear and she pressed her ear harder to his chest. She said, I'm sorry. People stared. *!PERFECT!* Jorge said something and it was either *I did it* or *I get it* and he walked away then, to the ball retriever, and he took his ball and rubbed it with a cloth he kept in his back pocket and he kissed it and then it was the sound of balls rolling, of pins exploding, of people laughing and joking as Split This! reanimated itself, kept going, people squeezing out the last few hours of game and companionship before returning home in cold cars to dark homes alone or together.

The Unicorn Has No Match…Or Mate. The Artist…Has No Peer.

Stephen Massimilla

Getting the world right is a dying operation. To see myself, I swivel
Tiny mirrors, piecing each feature together
One suture per second.
In poor sun, I bear witness
To a scar-pale coat in small clearing
Through skylight shaft, dust of the columbines sifting about,

Plums popping through skins beneath my hooves. Where the Muse
Would have posed, I draw her bodice so small
It stirrups breasts lit by interior bulbs. What is that

Edging the horn? *My God, it's blood*. She hears the rush
Of my head-toss
But won't unfold to feel my snow mane stroke
The neck's arch while
A man enters wearing—yes, it is—a green
Surgical mask and whispering to—an apprentice?—*this one's*

Been killing her foals. Not possible, but yes,
The low mound of abdomen
Is oozing sap. I know stupidly,

They are here to put down the mare. Her horn gores the ceiling,
But I have yet to draw the eyes.

As the apprentice bends in sky-lit scrubs
To touch a pencil brush,
I search the set, but the right blue is fly-by-
Day. The eyes are huge, tear-pooled, empty of pupils.

Why do I not have the proper blue? In the long run the draught of truth
Cannot not count, as I count to myself,
Not aloud, only

In my mind, in blank print, the animals said to weep
At the hour of their own dying.

The Wisdom of Dormancy

Corrie Williamson

To lose the scar of knowledge is to renew the wound.
—Wendell Berry

The trees raise battlements
of indulgent colors, day goes slender,
shadows setting their sharp ears to the ground.

In my bright living room I make gin
and tonics with the mint I carried here
in a terra cotta pot from half a country away.

In the land of those roots, my family counted
the winter dead like candles: days,
news, hours, the rising sun

dressing the beeches beyond
the glass in slim bony light. We read aloud
to them, sang, still—the flicker.

He tears leaves between his teeth
and kisses my mouth as if
spring could live in the tongue, as if

loss were not a perennial that blooms
in December, and I might forget
the slow muscling of its roots

the way a tree along a fence line
forgets, grows and seams
around the barbed wire's scar.

Splintered

Dakota Lyons

Confess

to the
burden
of
your

faces

I am drowning
in your

alias

the wrinkles
from
my
forehead

stripped
by footsteps

remnants of
red skies

and your

ling e r i n g

phrases

Messages From the Unseen World
(A Different Alan Turing And Me)

Ish Klein

Postcards for receptives

Differential equation— Science itself

Religion is boundary condition

the wall of which is firelike

No names Fixed widths become sick

Something happened you were not to appear

Rolling your eye through space and time

Exclusion principle was for the electrons themselves

who would be corrupted and become dragons or demons

from associating too freely

You say this arhythmic fount particle

how there could be (blanked) **I'm ready for retrieval**

Contributors' Biographies

Demosthenes Agrafiotis (1946), poet and intermedia artist, is active in the fields of poetry/ painting/ photography/ intermedia installations and their interactions, with books of poetry and essays, and exhibitions both in Greece and abroad. He has a special interest in the relations between art and new technologies. His book *Maribor* (The Post-Apollo Press) was awarded the 2011 Northern California Book Award for Poetry in Translation. *Chinese Notebook* (Ugly Duckling Presse) appeared later that same year. Both books are translated by Angelos and John Sakkis. His recent books are: *+-graphies* (Veer Books, London), *Betises* (Editions Fidel Anthelme X, Marseille, in French) and, *ArtxArt* (Redfoxpress, Ireland). He is based in Athens, Greece. **Suzanne Barnecut** is a Bay Area native, currently living in San Francisco with her husband and newborn daughter. She earned her MFA from California College of the Arts, and to date her work has appeared in *Slush Pile* and *Beeswax Magazine*. She is at work on a collection of stories and a first novel. **Allison Barret**t is a recent graduate of Cornell University's MFA program. Her poems have been published in *cream city review* and *ACREAGE*. She teaches English at Tompkins Cortland Community College and raises two kids under three. **Ace Boggess** is currently incarcerated in the West Virginia correctional system. His poetry has appeared in *Harvard Review, Mid-American Review, Notre Dame Review, River Styx, RATTLE, Atlanta Review* and other journals. His books include *The Beautiful Girl Whose Wish Was Not Fulfilled* (Highwire Press, 2003) and, as editor, *Wild Sweet Notes II,* an Anthology of West Virginia poetry (Publishers Place, 2004). **Michelle Carter**'s plays have received the Susan Glaspell Award, Backstage Garland Awards, the PEN West Award, and the PEN USA Literary Award in Drama. Her work has been produced and developed at theaters in San Francisco, Los Angeles, New York, Florida, Washington, New Jersey, and London, where she held a residency at the Donmar Theatre. She'll soon return to London to continue work on DREAMSPIEL: A Ukulele Opera, a collaboration with The Ukulele Orchestra of Great Britain. She has published short stories in many journals and anthologies as well as a novel with Penguin Books. **Doug Paul Case** lives in Bloomington, where he's an MFA candidate at Indiana University. His work is published or forthcoming in *Columbia Poetry Review, Pank, Wigleaf,* and others. He's probably wearing a cardigan. **MRB Chelko** holds an MFA from the University of New Hampshire and is Assistant Editor of the unbound poetry journal, *Tuesday; An Art Project*. Her recent work can be read online in *RealPoetik, POOL, Vinyl Poetry, Loaded Bicycle, Transom, Missouri Review,* and others. She lives in Harlem with her husband Nick, and dog Chuck, and has a daughter on the way. **Rick Crabtree** lives just outside of Batavia, OH, where he sleeps very little and spends as much time as possible with his two children, son 2, daughter 6. He is currently studying for degrees in English and Education at the University of Cincinnati Clifton campus. His work can also be found in *The Cobalt Review* and *Eastfork*, an online literary journal put out by the Clermont campus at the University of Cincinnati. Rick is a co-administrator for the Riverside Writer's Collective, a workshop group that meets in the village of Batavia. **Stacy Doris** is the author of *Kildare* (Roof, 1995), *Conference* (Potes & Poets, 2001), *Paramour* (Krupskaya, 2000), *Knot* (University of Georgia Press, 2006), *Cheerleader's Guide to the World: Council Book* (Roof Books, 2006), *The Cake Part* (Publication Studio, 2011) and *Fledge: A Phenomenology of Spirit* (Nightboat, 2012) in English, as well as books in French including *La Vie de Chester Steven Wiener écrite par sa femme* (P.O.L, 1998), *Une Année à New York avec Chester* (P.O.L, 2000), and *Parlement* (P.O.L, 2005). Internationally acclaimed poet, translator, and teacher, Doris died in San Francisco, California, on January 31, 2012. She had battled cancer (leiomyosarcoma) for the past three years. She was an Associate Professor in the Creative Writing Program of San Francisco State University, where she taught since 2002. 2011 American Book Award winner **Camille T. Dungy** is the author of three books, including *Smith Blue* and *Suck on the Marrow*, and the editor of anthologies including *Black Nature: Four Centuries of African American Nature Poetry* and *From the Fishouse: An Anthology of Poems that Sing, Rhyme, Resound, Syncopate, Alliterate, and Just Plain Sound Great.* Professor in the Creative Writing Department at San

Francisco State University, Dungy's honors include an NEA fellowship, two NACCP Image Award nominations, and two Northern California Book Awards. **Gail Rudd Entrekin** has taught Poetry and English Literature at California colleges for 25 years. Her collection of poems, *Change (Will Do You Good)* (Poetic Matrix Press), was nominated for a Northern California Book Award, and her new collection, *Rearrangement of the Invisible*, is forthcoming in 2012. Her poems were finalists for the Pablo Neruda Poetry Prize from *Nimrod* in 2011. She is editor of the online environmental literary journal *Canary* (www.hippocketpress.org/canary.cfm) and Poetry Editor of *Hip Pocket Press* in Orinda, California. **Rebecca Foust**'s books include *All That Gorgeous Pitiless Song* (Many Mountains Moving Book Prize, nominated for Poets' Prize, finalist for Paterson Prize) and *God, Seed* (2010 Foreword Book of the Year Award). Recent poems are in *Hudson Review, Notre Dame Review, Sewanee Review, Smartish Pace, Woman's Review of Books,* and elsewhere. **Matthew Gagnon** currently lives and works in western Massachusetts. His reviews and essays can be found in *Jacket, Jacket2, The Literary Review,* and *The Poker*, among others. Some of his poems have appeared or are forthcoming in *American Letters & Commentary, Boston Review, Colorado Review, Denver Quarterly, Hambone, The Nation,* and *Web Conjunctions.* **Ivan Hobson** received an MFA from San Francisco State University. He is a fourth-generation machinist, working in the small family shop his great-grandfather built in 1935. Metal working and family history has guided his poetry towards the sparks and shadows. Having his work appear in *Fourteen Hills* is a beautiful homecoming, one that comes with the recognition of Daniel Langton and Truong Tran for all the time they put in to help him grow. Ivan's poetry has recently appeared, or is forthcoming, in publications including the *South Dakota Review, The Fourth River, Plainsongs, Flyway,* and *Over the Transom*. Vancouver poet **Linda King** has published in numerous literary journals in Canada and internationally—*Event, CV2, Other Voices, The Toronto Quarterly, Lumina, Gargoyle.* Her work is upcoming in *The Pacific Poetry Project*, an anthology featuring poets from Portland, Seattle, and Vancouver. A graduate of The Writers' Studio at Simon Fraser University, King lives and writes near the beach. **Ish Klein** is the author of the poetry books *Moving Day* and *Union!* and a video collection *Success Window* (Poor

Claudia, 2011). Her work has screened at festivals and museums around the world. Video example: http://www.youtube.com/user/ishkleinfilms. She lives with Greg Purcell and they produce the *No Slander* poetry podcast: http://itunes.apple.com/us/podcast/the-no-slander-podcast/id419725253. **Dakota Lyons** was born and raised in Georgia. Having lived in the southern United States the majority of her life, this is where much of her inspiration comes from. She has been published in the University of Denver publication *Foothills* and has also received honorable mention at the Southern Women Writers Conference in Rome, Georgia. She is completing her senior year at the University of Denver, preparing to begin a Masters degree in English this coming fall. **Stephen Massimilla** is a poet, critic and painter. His collection, *Forty Floors from Yesterday*, received the Sonia Raiziss-Giop Bordighera Poetry Prize. Other awards include the Grolier Poetry Prize for *Later on Aiaia*, a Van Renssalaer Award, an Academy of American Poets Prize, and two Pushcart nominations. Massimilla has new work in *AGNI, Chelsea, The Colorado Review, Denver Quarterly, Green Mountains Review, Provincetown Arts, Quarterly West, Verse Daily,* and elsewhere. He teaches Classics and Modernist Literature at Columbia University. Website: stephenmassimilla.com **Kristi Moos** is the author of *Oakland Poems* (Deep Oakland, 2010) which won the Harold Taylor Prize from the Academy of American Poets. She is the founder and editor of *Poecology*, an online literary journal for writing about place and ecology. Her work has been published in *New American Writing; Denver Quarterly; San Diego City Works Press anthology Lavandería: A Mixed Load of Women, Wash, and Word; Im(prompt)u Review,* and elsewhere. She received her MFA in poetry from San Francisco State University. **Tom Oristaglio** lives in Brooklyn, New York, where he writes poetry and molests photocopy machines in his spare time. His poems have appeared in *Armchair/Shotgun, Cricket Online Review, Anatomy & Etymology,* and *Rabbit Catastrophe*. **Eliza Rotterman**'s poetry and reviews have appeared or are forthcoming in *Zoland, Hubbub,* and *Poetry International.* She recently was the recipient of the Henry David Thoreau Fellowship from The Vermont Studio Center. She lives in Portland, Oregon, where she is studying to become a nurse. **Angelos Sakkis** was born in Pireus, Greece. He studied design in Athens and worked for a time as an assistant to the painter Spyros Vassiliou. After he immigrated to U.S in 1970, he recieved his BFA from San Francisco Art Institute in 1989. His work is in collections in Greece and California. A chapbook, *Travel Log With Homer On My Mind,* appeared from BOTH BOTH Books in 2012. With John Sakkis he has translated the work of poet/multi-media artist Demosthenes Agrafiotis. His poetry has appeared in *Ambush review* and *try chap-mag.* He lives in Oakland, California. **John Sakkis** is the author of *Rude Girl* (BlazeVOX Books), and with Angelos Sakkis he has translated two books by Athenian poet and multi-media artist Demosthenes Agrafiotis—*Maribor* (The Post-Apollo Press), awarded the 2011 Northern California Book Award for Poetry in Translation, and *Chinese Notebook* (Ugly Duckling Presse). He is the author of numerous chapbooks, pamphlets, mixtapes and ephemera, most recently *RAVE ON!* (Lew Gallery). Under the moniker BOTH BOTH he has curated/ edited various projects including: blog, "band," reading series, and since 2005, a magazine. A graduate of San Francisco State University and Naropa University, he lives in Oakland. **Michael Sandler** has other new work appearing in *Moment Magazine, Ducts, Glass: A Journal of Poetry, The Puritan, Peregrine, Diverse Voices Quarterly, California Quarterly, Natural Bridge,* and *Ship of Fools.* He lives near Seattle where he also works as an arbitrator. **Peter Stenson** is the author of the novel *Shadows and Aphrodisiacs* (forthcoming from Crown in 2013). He has stories and essays published or forthcoming in *The Sun, Confrontation, Post Road, Fugue, Passages North, The Pinch, Blue Mesa Review,* and *Upstreet*, among others. He has been nominated for a Pushcart Prize. He is currently working on his MFA in fiction at Colorado State University. **Rutherford Sullivan** lives in Chattanooga, Tennessee, because the rent is cheap and the food is decent. He studies English at the University of Tennessee at Chattanooga and is currently at work on his first novel, due next year. **Siamak Vossoughi** was born in Tehran, Iran in 1972, and grew up in London, Orange County, and Seattle. He attended the University of Washington, majoring in English. He came to San Francisco in 1994, when he began working at Presidio Hill School in various capacities. He has been writing short stories with hopes of writing novels and plays. He has had stories published in *Faultline,*

Konch Magazine, and *A River & Sound Review.* Much of his work can also be found at www.iranian.com. His main feeling about a short story is that a reader ought to feel more glad to be alive, even with all the trouble in life, after they read it than they did before. **Kate Warne** lives and writes in Berkeley, California. She is an MFA candidate in poetry at San Francisco State University. **Lauren Waterman**'s fiction has appeared in the online literary magazines *Anderbo* and *Monkeybicycle;* her non fiction has been featured in *Vogue, InStyle, Boston,* and *New York.* Raised in Virginia, she currently lives in Brooklyn with her husband, and she is working on her first novel. A native of Virginia, **Corrie Williamson** is an MFA candidate in poetry at the University of Arkansas, where she has taught, served as director of the Writers in the Schools Program, and is the current Walton Fellow in Poetry. Her poems have recently appeared or are forthcoming in *The Southeast Review, cream city review, 32 Poems, Smartish Pace*, and elsewhere. **John Yearley** is the author of *Leap*, winner of the Mickey Kaplan New American Play Prize (Cincinnati Playhouse in the Park, Abingdon Theatre), and *Ephemera*, winner of the John Gassner Award (Summer Play Festival, LABryinth Intensive). His plays *A Low-Lying Fog* and *All in Little Pieces* are published by Samuel French. He has worked as a "script doctor" for New Line Cinema, and developed the animated series *Mamu & Dinga.* His new play, *Another Girl*, was read at Naked Angels and selected for the PlayPenn festival in 21011. Author of the forthcoming book *Daddy's Not Tall Enough to Touch the Moon.* Member of the Writers Guild of America, the Dramatists Guild, and a MacDowell Fellow.

The Editors would like to thank the following bookstores for carrying *Fourteen Hills*:

In the Bay Area:

Adobe Books
Aardvark Books
Alexander Books Co.
Analog Books
Bird and Becket
Books and Bookshelves
Books, Inc.
Booksmith
Bound Together Books
Christopher's Books
City Lights
Diesel Bookstore
Dog Eared Books
Eastwind Books Berkeley
Farley's
Green Apple
Issues
Main Street Cafe and Books
Modern Times
Needles & Pens
Pegasus and Pendragon
Phoenix Books
SFSU Bookstore
Smoke Signals
University Press Books
USF Bookstore
Walden Pond Books
West Portal Bookshop

In California:

Bookstore Benicia :: Benicia
Bookshop Santa Cruz :: Santa Cruz
Captiola Book Cafe :: Santa Cruz
Copperfield's Books :: Petaluma
Kepler's :: Menlo Park
Main Street Books :: Los Altos
Reader's Books :: Sonoma
Sawyer's News :: Santa Rosa
Watershed Books :: Lakeport
William Jessup University :: Rocklin

Across the U.S.:

57th Street Bookstore :: Chicago, IL
Atomic Books :: Baltimore, MD
Avril 50 :: Philidelphia, PA
Book Corner :: Bloomington, IN
Chicago Main Newsstand :: Evanston, IL
Crescent Tobacco Shop :: Tucson, AZ
Hudson News Grand Central :: NY, NY
Ink On A :: NY, NY
Magazine Cafe :: NY, NY
Magpies Newstand Cafe :: Durango, CO
McNally Jackson Books :: NY, NY
Newsbreak Swansea :: Swansea, MA
Newsland Alburquerque :: Alburquerque, NM
Nick Smoke Magazine :: NY, NY
Paras News :: NY, NY
Praire Lights :: Iowa City, IA
Quimby's Books :: Chicago, IL
Regulator Bookshop :: Durham, NC
Sam Weller's Zion Bookshop :: Salt Lake City, UT
St. Marks Books :: NY, NY
Tattered Cover Books Cherry Creek :: Denver, CO
Union Square Magazine Shop :: NY, NY
Universal News Broadway :: NY, NY
University Bookstore Wisconsin :: Madison, WI
Women and Children First :: Chicago, IL
Writer's Center :: Chicago, IL
Writer's Center :: Bethesda, MD

1111:
Writing
and Art that
Dances!
Submit!
Eleven Eleven: A Journal of Literature and Art
California College of the Arts
1111 Eighth Street
San Francisco, California 94107
elevenelevenjournal.com

www.santaclarareview.com

NEWS
Dec 29, 2004 - The Inkscape developers have set a goal for the release of Inkscape 0.41 for mid-late January. There are some noteworthy new features that would be worth getting out to users, and with some major internal changes that will be taking place soon, a good stable release is needed prior to starting such an undertaking.
Current
NOW ACCEPTING SUBMISSIONS FOR ISSUE 16
Switchback
DEADLINE 8.31.12
www.swback.com
SWITCHBACK IS A PUBLICATION OF THE MFA PROGRAM AT THE UNIVERSITY OF SAN FRANCISCO

Subscribe to Fourteen Hills

Please circle one. Prices include shipping and handling.

Single issue (current): $9

One Year (two issues): $15

Two Years (four issues): $28

Institutional (one year): $17

Back Issues (please specify): $5

Volume______No.______Qty____

Name____

Street Address_________________________________

City___________________ State/Province______________

Zip/ Postal code_________ Country___________________

Phone_________________ E-mail_____________________

Please enclose a check payable to Fourteen Hills: The SFSU Review and mail to :
Fourteen Hills
Department of Creative Writing
San Francisco State University
1600 Holloway Avenue
San Francisco, CA 94132-1722

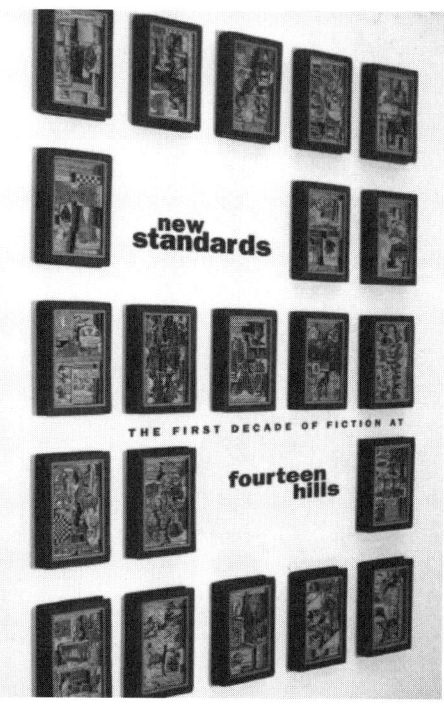

An anthology commemorating Fourteen Hills' ongoing dedication to innovative fiction.

Stephen Elliott, Peter Orner, Eireene Nealand, Pam Houston, Robert Glück
Nona Caspers, John Cleary, Pamela Ryder, and many more

Price (shipping and handling included): $15.00 Qty______
Name__________________________________
Street Address____________________________
City________________ State/Province_____________
Zip/Postal Code________ Country________________
Phone________________ E-mail__________________

Also available on Amazon or from Small Press Distribution
www.spdbooks.org